WHAT SAYING ABOUT

Catch the Wind of the Spirit...

"Carolyn Tennant has again challenged the church with a prophetic and practical voice through the currents of the wind of the Spirit. Her spiritual insights and rich usage of revival and church history are intriguing and catching. She is a humble leader with a powerful word for the church and her leaders in the twenty-first century. This is a must-read for those hungering for the wind of the Spirit to blow once again in the American church."

—Joseph S. Girdler, superintendent, Kentucky Ministry Network, Assemblies of God

"For many years Carolyn Tennant has been an example and inspiration to thousands of students at North Central University. For as long as I've known her, she's been a proponent of spiritual revitalization in the church. To all who know her, she models prayer and listening to the Lord. Her book leads each of us to a deeper understanding of our gifts and callings. Reading this book has challenged me to be more attentive to the Spirit's leading. Carolyn has a passion for the church to have a greater balance of the five-fold ministry. When that happens, there will be a great spiritual awakening in the church. It is my prayer that all across our nation and around the globe, this will be the case."

—Clarence St. John, superintendent, Minnesota Ministry Network, Assemblies of God

"Carolyn brilliantly sums up the choice before the North American church today: stay stagnant and passive on the shore or ride the currents of the Holy Spirit into the fullness of God's purpose for this generation, jealously guarding the ancient truths while being open to fresh moves of the Spirit. Out of the treasury of her rich experience as a teacher, author, minister, and passionate seeker after God, she pleads for an authentic restoration of the things that made the early church such a game-changer. If you are serious about the church, and your role in it, this is the book you have been waiting for."

—Dennis Ignatius, former Malaysian Ambassador to Canada

"I've worked with my friend Carolyn Tennant for over thirty years and have been blessed by her spiritual insights and wisdom on how to apply biblical principles to life and leadership. Her work on revivals and the fivefold ministry gifts is outstanding and is a much needed contribution to the ministry of the church in these days. Carolyn understands the rigors of practical leadership and how to be a truly revived person in the midst of difficult circumstances. Thank you, Carolyn, for helping us see how the Spirit provides supernatural power and gifts to change real-life situations!"

—Dr. Gordon Anderson, president, North Central University, Minneapolis, MN

"Dr. Tennant brings her seasoned prophetic voice as well as her distinguished academic credentials to the discussion/debate concerning fivefold ministry. Make no mistake about it—this is not a rehashing of old arguments but a creative perspective from the heart of a historian and revivalist. If you are looking for practical insights and application, this is your book. Warning: buckle your seat belts; prepare to be stretched!"

—Al and Deb Warner, Set Free Inc., Buffalo, NY, www.setfreeleaders.com

"Dr. Tennant has received a Word from the Lord concerning the fivefold gifts Christ has given the church. The cure for the dysfunctions in the American church is found in a return to the five-fold ministry pattern found in Ephesians 4:11. Dr. Tennant helps us solidify and strengthen these five offices. We will do more than survive, but thrive."

—Donald Gifford, superintendent, Indiana District Assemblies of God

"Carolyn has been a friend and mentor for many years. Her writings have profoundly impacted our lives and those of our students at the Bible School here in Argentina. This book is what we've felt but haven't been able to put into words—a practical way to live daily, functioning in what we've been born to be in Christ."

—Sherry Grams, missionary to Argentina

"Carolyn Tennant writes from the perspective of a person who has lived and experienced the ministry of the Holy Spirit in her own life in an enormous variety of venues: from local churches, to the university campus, to classes in which she has shared her insight with many pastors and recognized church leaders. She is not an armchair theologian nor is she a fly-by-night, eclectic, self-taught opinion giver. She knows the Word, the church and the need. Her words resonate as we face the enormous challenges of our day."

—Rocky Grams, president, River Plate Bible College, Lomas, Argentina

"The postmodern air we breathe tends to numb us to the fact that faithful followers of Jesus have been traversing their own contemporary challenges for centuries. We aren't the first to face formidable opposition to our faith nor are our strategies so original as to be deemed cutting edge. Carolyn Tennant offers insights to those who have a hunch that the usual suspects (called by some experts) about church growth and revitalization are all too often drinking at the same well, which shamelessly offers shallow inspiration and short-term solutions veiled in hipster clothing. Dr. Tennant does the unthinkable: she takes church history seriously and the Bible authoritatively. The resulting volume is an introduction to lives of the saints who are worth emulating. The key passages thoroughly investigated in Paul's writings to the Ephesians are not mere proof texts for her theories on church revitalization, but study that yields "lamps unto our feet and light unto our pathways.'"

—Byron D. Klaus, president, Assemblies of God Theological Seminary (1999–2015)

"Dr. Tennant offers the reader the yield of a lifetime of study, contemplation, prayer, and service, which flow from her commitment to Christian thought and ministry. She has produced a trove of wisdom, tried and tested in the acid bath of experience. 'Without an oar' but 'carried on the current' is the call Dr. Tennant urges the reader to consider on the ministry journey. She sets her premise on the early Celtic missional tradition of boarding a coracle, a small rudderless vessel, and trusting the impetus of God's provision to take it to the destination He directs. She challenges the evangelist, teacher, pastor, prophet, and apostle to lean into the wind, trust the current, and follow the manifest—biblical principles and the compass of the Spirit. God provides the direction, speed, and destination of the journey. I'm ready to set sail! This book has aroused in me the desire to be more sensitive to the prompting of the current. Ahoy and Godspeed!"

—Judy Rachels, network director, National Women in Ministry Network of the Assemblies of God

"'I love humanity. It's people I can't stand.' This comment was supposedly shared by a very frustrated pastor. Serving as pastors and leaders, people are all we have to work with. People can be the joy of ministry or the source of great pain. Dr. Tennant presents a laser focus on ministering to individuals. In church life we have a tendency to elevate leaders and strive for bigger numbers and larger buildings. These are all good if they aren't primary. The New Testament is clear, individuals/people are the priority. This book presents a much-needed, practical encouragement on how the gifts of the Holy Spirit can positively minister to and through individuals so they can carry out the New Testament mandate 'to do the work of the ministry.' As a result the Great Commission to 'go into all the world and preach the gospel' is actualized."

—Don Argue, EdD, ambassador at large for Convoy of Hope; president, Northwest University (1998–2007)

"Dr. Carolyn Tennant is an apostolic professor and practitioner of revival. Her anointed ministry in the pulpits of America, Europe, and Argentina brings a fresh wind of the Spirit. *Catch the Wind of the Spirit* will powerfully move the reader into the five ministry gifts she describes. For seekers of revival this book will be a great inspiration."

—David and Beth Grant, cofounders of Project Rescue

"When it comes to having a voice of authority about the things of God and His beloved church, Dr. Carolyn Tennant has both the academic and ministry-experience chops to earn a serious hearing. In this masterful and comprehensive look at the five ministry gifts and their corresponding currents, she delivers fresh spiritual insights with passion and heart. But this is what matters most: the truths she unfolds have the potential to revolutionize both individual believers and also how the body of Christ impacts our planet. Carolyn isn't afraid of the deep end. She knows firsthand that the God-currents there will take us on remarkable adventures where Jesus is glorified and lives are forever changed. After reading *Catch the Wind of the Spirit*, my heart is longing to climb into the next coracle and head for deeper waters myself. Read this book and get ready to ride the current into your own God-adventure!"

—Jodi Detrick, DMin, writer, speaker, coach, mentor, author of *The Jesus-Hearted Woman*

CATCH
the
WIND
of the
SPIRIT

How the 5 Ministry Gifts Can Transform Your Church

CAROLYN TENNANT

Copyright © 2016 by Carolyn Tennant

ALL RIGHTS RESERVED

Published by Vital Resources

1445 N. Boonville Ave.

Springfield, Missouri 65802

No portion of this book may be reproduced, stored in a retrieval system, or transmitted in any form or by any means—electronic, mechanical, photocopy, recording, or any other—except for brief quotations in printed reviews, without the prior written permission of the publisher.

Cover design and interior formatting by Prodigy Pixel (www.prodigypixel.com)

Unless otherwise specified, Scripture quotations used in this book are taken from the 2011 edition of the Holy Bible, New International Version®. NIV®. Copyright © 1973, 1978, 1984, 2011 by Biblica, Inc. ™ Used by permission of Zondervan. All rights reserved worldwide.www.zondervan.com. The "NIV" and "New International Version" are trademarks registered in the United States Patent and Trademark Office by Biblica, Inc.™

Scriptures marked NRSV are from the New Revised Standard Version of the Bible. © 1989 by the Division of Christian Education of the National Council of the Churches of Christ in the U.S.A. Used by permission. All rights reserved.

Scriptures marked NKJV are from THE NEW KING JAMES VERSION®. © 1982 by Thomas Nelson, Inc. Used by permission. All rights reserved.

Scriptures marked ASV are from the American Standard Version of the Bible which is held in public domain in the United States.

ISBN: 978-1-68066-038-8

Printed in the United States of America

19 18 17 16 • 1 2 3 4 5

THIS BOOK IS LOVINGLY DEDICATED TO

Ray Tennant, who has been a steady partner in our coracle. He is committed to catching the Wind and the currents, and this has been a great treasure.

CONTENTS

Foreword

Introduction

Chapter 1	Living on a Coracle
Chapter 2	Jesus Gives Gifts to the Church
Chapter 3	The Powerful Wooing Current
Chapter 4	The Evangelist
Chapter 5	The Radical Forming Current
Chapter 6	The Teacher
Chapter 7	The Synchronized Choreography Current
Chapter 8	The Pastor
Chapter 9	The Directional Prophetic Current
Chapter 10	The Prophetic Servant
Chapter 11	The Miraculous Sending Current
Chapter 12	The Apostolic Emissary
Chapter 13	We Shall Not Cease from Exploration
Chapter 14	Let's Chat

Endnotes

About the Author

FOREWORD

I grew up loving the church. Encounters with God, Christ-centered preaching, remarkable people, miracle testimonies, awe-inspiring worship—there was and is so much to love! Truly, no place, no organization, no community anywhere in the world is like Christ's living church. The apostle Paul described it as a human "sanctuary" where God dwells (Eph. 2:22). The church is God's chosen, living habitation in the earth.

Yet, in spite of its wonder and potential, I carry a deep concern for the church's health and vitality as we in the Western world push further into the twenty-first century. Christianity's center of gravity has shifted largely to the Global South. Meanwhile, the church in many places in the west seems lethargic, increasingly powerless against the headwinds of cultural secularism, religious pluralism, moral relativism, and aggressive atheism.

There has also been a concurrent "love Jesus, hate church" cynicism growing among an increasing number of Christian believers—a cynicism born out of disillusionment with superficial, predictable, impersonal forms of church life. Yet spiritual hunger runs rampant in the secular culture. Either these are the shadows of death or foreshadows of one more spiritual awakening in the land before Christ returns.

In this sweepingly comprehensive book, Carolyn Tennant outlines a prescription for Spirit-empowered church health realized through the dynamics of the five leadership gifts of Ephesians 4. She deftly and intentionally sidesteps the controversies commonly associated with these ministry gifts, focusing instead on Holy Spirit flow giving place to spiritual function and transformational ministry. The result is health for the whole church.

Behind each page is the Carolyn I remember during my years as a campus ministry pastor. We would periodically partner on student discipleship projects at North Central University. I found Carolyn to be a person who blends a deep personal spirituality with a passionate commitment to the Spirit's supernatural, formational activity in people's lives. Her life experience, her sensitivity to the voice of the Spirit, and her broad influence bring depth and credibility to this work.

I firmly believe that Jesus does, indeed, want to restore health, vitality, and authority to His church before He comes again. Read with an ear to the Spirit and respond with faith that you can be part of Christ's church revived in our day.

—James Bradford, general secretary, The General Council of the Assemblies of God

INTRODUCTION

The cry for renewal and revitalization in the church today is high. We're in a crisis moment. The church is trying to understand and adjust to the massive societal shifts that are occurring all around us.

Concurrently, individual Christians are crying out for more meaning in their spiritual lives. They also want to be rejuvenated, but many of the avenues available to them seem pointless. Where do they go to satisfy their hearts' cry?

Catch the Wind of the Spirit grew out of this context of need and emanated from a deep study of Ephesians 4. After pondering the five ministry gifts for years, I've come to the conclusion that our emphasis has been all wrong. The vast majority of teaching on this has focused on church leadership. I'm firmly convinced, however, that God is focused upon the ministry currents that each person is supposed to oversee. He means for the whole church to get involved.

It has never really been all about the leader, has it? It's always been about what God is doing. So this book takes us on a different route than others that have been written on this subject. We first look at what God wants to accomplish and the potential strength He desires in each area. I am calling each of the gifts a "current" since I believe God wants to see each one flow freely and powerfully in the church, originating and being guided from the throne room of God. These five gifts or currents consist of the following:

1. Seeing people come to Christ (The Powerful Wooing Current)
2. Ensuring new believers learn to follow Him closely and mature into what He desires them to be (The Radical Forming Current)
3. Caring for His disciples in the body of believers so they stay healthy, and connected, and know they are loved (The Synchronized Choreography Current)
4. Providing direction for the church: correcting and restoring, affirming and encouraging (The Housecleaning Directional Current)
5. Pushing back the darkness and taking new territory for the kingdom of God (The Miraculous Sending Current)

Right now the currents are not flowing at the strength they could be. The chapter for each current discusses what a free flow of God's Spirit would actually look like. It considers how every member of the Trinity has been involved in each current. Usually, a little historical perspective is offered to indicate periods of time when that current was on the move. I also provide a Scriptural basis to help us gain a deeper understanding of what the Lord might want for us. Then I propose possible changes and shifts for individuals and for the church.

Each "current" chapter is followed by its twin: a chapter that considers what kind of people are needed to oversee that current and where they might be in our churches. These chapters consider the role of evangelist, teacher, and pastor as well as the work of the prophetic and apostolic role. We will discuss misconceptions for some of these roles (especially the last two), ending in a biblical perspective of what God may be wanting to see in the church today.

The book closes with a consideration of how all this might apply in the church today. What implications does it have for the inner workings and oversight of the church? Truly it is my fondest hope that throughout you are drawn closer to the Father, Son, and Holy Spirit.

Since I'm a storyteller by nature, you'll discover many stories, illustrations, quotes, and applications of the principles we'll consider. My special interests in Celtic church history from St. Patrick on will come through, along with my lifetime study of historical church revivals. I enjoy weaving themes and symbolism in and out, like a Celtic knot. So if you go with me on this journey, I guarantee you'll find some twists and turns. Just join the ride.

The British poet T. S. Elliot (1888–1965) wrote pieces I particularly enjoy after he became a believer in Christ. In his poem "Little Gidding" from the longer work *Four Quartets* he wrote this:

> We shall not cease from exploration
>
> And the end of all our exploring
>
> Will be to arrive where we started
>
> And know the place for the first time.[1]

I hope when you close the covers of this book, you will see some things differently than you did when you started. Happy journeying . . . the subject of chapter one.

Chapter One

LIVING ON A CORACLE

In the days of the ancient Celtic church, (AD 430 to about 900), one could see some exciting ventures on the high seas. The Welsh, Irish, and Scottish had long been making small boats from which they would launch into the sea to fish and move from place to place.

Called a coracle (or *currach* in Scotch Gaelic), the boat was generally designed for one or two people and was in the shape of a walnut shell. Split willow rods were bent and interwoven to form a frame. Then this was covered with animal hide and the seams were tarred. The boats were light and easy to carry from place to place. Generally they were propelled by broad-bladed paddles.

The Celtic monks were by no means opposed to adventure, and they liked to build larger coracles that would hold more people and set out into the ocean. This would be adventurous by itself, but additionally the coracles were rudderless and often the monks would take no oars or paddles. They hoisted their sails and caught the winds and the currents, believing that God would take them where they were supposed to go to share the gospel.

Once I had the opportunity to set off into the Atlantic Ocean in a fairly small fisherman's boat to visit the island of Skellig Michael, an ancient and famous monastic prayer settlement off the coast of Kerry in southwest Ireland. My students and I were all drenched after the twelve kilometers braving the waves, in spite of being given tarps. The reality of setting out into the ocean without oars is indeed monumental!

The monks (of course, Protestantism did not yet exist) would prepare carefully for such an expedition, especially in prayer and fasting. One such venture blew the missionaries from Ireland to the southern tip of Cornwall. The king of the area where they finally landed came out to greet them and was appalled that the monks had no oars. He decided to put his faith in the God the monks trusted so completely, and most of the rest of the tribe did the same.

Other monks built hermit huts or prayer cells or monasteries where they landed. People would inevitably gather around these men and women of God, and vibrant communities of faith would rise up. Many examples exist, but I vividly remember seeing for the first time the famous Irish Celtic church foundation of Iona, which was established by Columba as a vital missions point for Scotland.

The prayer history on that island has been so intense that people popularly say there is a "thin veil between heaven and earth." Surely I can attest to the powerful presence of the Lord, and there I was, coming to Iona by boat on the very day (the day before Pentecost Sunday) that Columba had arrived in his coracle for the first time in AD 563. He named that beach where he landed Port a Churaich, or the Haven of the Coracles.

Another famous coracle journey was by Brendan of Clonfert (c. AD 484–577) who built a coracle large enough to hold fourteen to seventeen monks. In this traditional hide-covered vessel—this time with oars and a rudder—Brendan and his crew traveled on a seven-year journey that took them to Iceland and ultimately Newfoundland. Possibly they got as far south as Florida because of the kind of fruit Brendan described, making him a precursor to Columbus, who visited Brendan's monastery to look over his maps. A book about this journey became the European bestseller of its day for years and years: V*oyage of St. Brendan the Abbot.*

I believe the Lord is asking us today, both as individuals and as the church corporately, to set sail again—to trust Him. He is wondering if we are willing to pull in our rudders and even throw away our oars and let the wind blow through our sails.

Jesus said, "The wind blows wherever it pleases. You hear its sound, but you cannot tell where it comes from or where it is going. So it is with everything born of the Spirit" (John 3:8). This picture of Christians who are born of the Spirit is an enticing one. Jesus is basically saying that we are free to move and journey from place to place, not only physically but also in our spirits.

The Irish took this literally and were committed to going on what they called *peregrinatio*, which means travel/pilgrimage. They did this wholeheartedly, taking the gospel throughout Europe to become one of the greatest and most effective mission movements of all time. However, the pilgrimage was also personal.

In *The Celtic Way*, Ian Bradley notes, "Peregrinatio was the outward symbol of an inner change, a metaphor and a symbol for the journey towards deeper faith and greater holiness and that journey toward God which is the Christian life."[2] Bradley also says that the purpose and goal of pilgrimage was "seeking the place of one's resurrection."[3]

JOURNEYING BY WIND AND CURRENTS

Our Christian lives should be viewed as a journey, a seeking, an opportunity for growth and transformation. At the end of it all, we will have a resurrection to eternal life, but God wants to bring us vivacity and renewal along the way as we travel through life. It appears to me that too many Christians, and also too many churches, have simply gotten stuck. They're in a rut instead of on a journey.

The reason I think this to be true is not simply observation. Rather, people tell me this so often that I'm becoming distressed by the trend. They feel they aren't growing as they wish. Church life seems boring, they say. "We do the same thing over and over, and even the faddish changes seem pointless. We aren't going anywhere." People want to be on the move!

God has provided currents for us to catch. However, if the currents have been stopped up, we will be sitting still. We have rocks and debris that have gathered at the source of the spring that are hindering the free flow of what God wants to do. These important currents need to be invigorated to the level of strength that God designed. God wants to give and restore these five currents or ministry gifts and the complete leadership team that oversees them. He wants the whole church involved because these currents are His primary values for *all* of us.

Following Jesus is a journey. It demands movement and change, action and courage. Any journey involves some sort of risk and adventure. We have to move outside of our comfort zones and head into the unknown. God is calling His church right now to move out with Him. Where will the wind and the currents take us? We don't know, but this doesn't mean we can be excused from moving.

When the tide is rising and going out, everyone must choose. Will we stay on shore or will we jump in? If we put one leg in the coracle and then hesitate, the coracle will have us doing the splits in no time. We have to seize the moment and take off . . . or not.

Too many of us have decided to stay on shore, while the Spirit wants to take us on a ride. We tend to have a preference for the known over the unknown. How much more comfortable it is to play it safe. But what are we missing? We will never reach the new place God has in mind if we don't hop in and go for the ride.

George Macleod, founder of the present-day Iona Community in 1936, made this comment:

Christ is a person to be trusted, not a principle to be tested. The Church is Movement, not a meeting house. The Faith is an Experience, not an exposition. Christians are Explorers, not map makers. It is a present Experience made possible at Bethlehem, offered on Calvary, and communicated at Pentecost.[4]

Indeed, if we are ever called upon to make maps, we have to explore first. We must get up and launch forth. Jesus is ready to experience the wind and the waves with us. He will be in the boat and our faith will be built. We lose testimonies of His faithfulness if we do not take risks.

If Daniel had not continued to pray to God instead of King Darius, he would not have seen the miracle of the lions' den. If Shadrach, Meshach, and Abednego had not refused to bow down to the golden image, they would not have been saved from the fiery furnace. If Queen Esther had not risked her life to go in to King Ahasuerus, her people would not have been saved. God has given us His Word full of stories, not just a list of principles, because the main point is to put principles into action. Indeed, stories of faith require risk and setting out into the unknown, but then we see God come through!

Brendan the Navigator was constantly encouraging his fellow monks to trust in God and have faith:

> After fifteen days the wind dropped and they set themselves to the oars until their strength failed. Straightaway Saint Brendan began to comfort and encourage them, saying: "Brothers, do not fear, for God is our helper, our helmsman and our pilot, and he shall guide us. Pull in all the oars and the rudder. Just leave the sails spread, and let God do as he wishes with his servants and their boat." Then they continued to refresh their strength until the evening, as long as the wind did not cease to blow. Still, they could not tell from which direction the wind came or in which direction the boat was carried.[5]

Whether the wind of God is particularly active or not, as we wait on Him, we renew our strength to continue our journeys. He is most assuredly our pilot and wants to decide where we go, when we go, and how we go. This reliance on Him and obedience to His plans, ways, and timing are an essential part of what God desires to do today to renew His people and revitalize the church as a whole.

We were not meant to look to our own strength or attempt to make everything look more fashionable. Even the best looking boat in the world can capsize. What we need so desperately is God, the instigator of the wind of the Spirit and the prime mover of the currents of the church. When we feel out of control, He is definitely in control as we put our trust in Him. Often all that is expected of us is to be silent, rest in Him, and place our faith in the Helmsman.

I'm convinced that if we want to see church revitalization, this must be our posture. It is time for an adventure rather than playing it safe. Instead of thinking of the church so much as an organization, we need to think of ourselves as being on a journey with other pilgrims. Our leader is God. We have to stay close to Him or we will lose sight of where He is taking us right now. Sometimes it seems easier to keep our eyes on where He was yesterday than where He is today.

The late Irish poet John O'Donohue wrote this lovely little poem, which ironically provides a huge perspective on life:

FLUENT

I would love to live

Like a river flows

Carried by the surprise

Of its own unfolding.[6]

God wants us to flow along with Him, bouncing in the currents that He generates (not the ones society spawns) and being swept up in the wind that He blows. He longs to surprise us. Jesus wants us to experience the thrill of following Him and growing into His likeness. How do we live in a post-Christian society? Like Christ. End of sermon.

Journeys have always been part of God's plan. Consider Abraham and Sarah setting out for the promised land, Jacob and his treks, Moses and the Hebrew people wandering in the wilderness, Mary and Joseph going to Egypt, Paul's missionary journeys . . . there are so many examples. God keeps saying, "Go!" and we keep saying, "But I'm comfortable where I am. Not now."

When Jesus said in John 14:6 that He was "the way and the truth and the life," He meant that no one could find the Father apart from Him. However, this certainly means following Him on whatever way He calls us to go. Jesus didn't intend for us to become stagnant. To be Christian means to be a person who is on the way, a church that is on the move. There is never a sense of arrival, but rather a process of being, becoming, changing, and overcoming.

ADVENTURING

It's impossible to know what we're even looking for until we venture forth. We have this deep haunting feeling that there is more, but what exactly? Until we set out, we can't completely discover who we are. What is inside of us must be tested. Our potential has to be plumbed.

We all have to reach inside and find both the good and the bad that is there before we can hand it all over to the Lord to change. God doesn't expect us to tidy up everything and present Him with a perfect self. He knows us completely and wants to be an integral part of the process of transformation. He intends to be on the journey with us.

The Celtic church prayed a great deal, and this launched them on their journeys. Prayer has to be the basis for launching out, otherwise we'll mistake wanderlust for God's movement.

A remarkable example of this foundation of prayer was the Skellig Michael prayer community that I earlier referred to visiting. Established somewhere between the sixth and eighth centuries, it lasted into the twelfth or thirteenth centuries. This is a crag of a rock island in the Atlantic with 640 rock steps built by the monks into the steep rise. As we climbed the steps, they took us to a rock terrace 600 feet above the water where twelve monks lived in six rock corbelled "beehive" huts. Here they prayed in two oratories because their whole purpose was to be able to concentrate so they could "fight the Devil."

The monks lived on birds' eggs, fish, vegetables from their little garden, and rainwater. All food was eaten raw; no wood existed on the island. The wintertime must have been formidable. Nonetheless, for hundreds of years twelve monks lived on this island. When one passed away, another was allowed to take his place. Celtic crosses mark their small graveyard.

I believe prayer is dwindling among us. Could we find even one person so committed to it that they would eat raw fish eggs on an isolated island in the middle of nowhere—even for a week, let alone a lifetime? Could we find twelve? Certainly while these men were praying, Christianity spread. Irish monks took Christianity up into Scotland, Britain, and to the barbaric tribes all over Europe. Would you or I even be here as Christians today if those men and other believers like them hadn't prayed? In order for the church to be on the move, prayer is essential. It is how we catch the wind.

As the postmodern church moves beyond petition to ask what is on God's heart, I believe that we, too, will be called forth into new places. God will not ask all of us to be missionaries, but He will summon us to venture out of our ruts—and the church will find renewal. This will be God's doing, and it will massively affect our postmodern society.

The church is meant to be the on-going presence of God in the world through union with Christ and the power of the Spirit. Following Jesus was an exciting activity in Bible times, and it still is today. He was and is cross-cultural, counter-cultural, and surprising. When the wind of the Spirit blows, He will take us into some unusual escapades, but following Him is always worth it. That is the only way we will truly be able to impact our society today.

RESTORING COURAGE

If the Celtic church could comment upon the present-day church, they would probably wonder at us. From their vantage point, they would likely say that we are boring and accuse us of letting fear and malaise hold us back. Real life with Jesus is never boring. When we follow Him, we will be challenged; there will be storms and raging seas. As we stay close to Him, however, He will guide us through.

Jesus' journey on earth took Him down a courageous path. Following the Father meant He would do some unconventional things. He would heal on the Sabbath, overturn the money changers' tables in the temple area, and spit in a man's blind eyes so he would be healed.

Jesus cast a possessed man's legion of demons into a nearby herd of 2,000 pigs, resulting in their going haywire and running into the lake to drown themselves (Mark 5:1–20). I can only imagine what environmentalists would say to that cleanup job! The townspeople were happy, of course, that the demoniac was clothed and in his right mind. No! They were afraid and asked Jesus to leave the region. Not a good precursor to church growth, eh?

Really, I wonder if we would still be considered respectable members of our churches if we accomplished just 10 percent of what Jesus did. Surely the Pharisees and Sadducees weren't excited about His methods. He was so out-of-the-box that they finally just wanted Him out of the way.

The church is trying to grab people's attention today, but we're attempting to do it from inside the box. We want everything to be in order and appealing according to society's standards. If the church is to be restored and revitalized, it must first decide that it will do everything God's way. Not a few things but *everything*. This is much easier said than done.

We feel we know what society needs and wants so surely that must be what the Lord wants. We move ahead and implement our ideas. We mean well, but is it God's way to accomplish what He desires? An old Yiddish proverb says, "If you want to make God laugh, tell Him your plans." Rather than telling Him all about our plans and asking Him to bless them, we need to hear His plans.

The Lord reminds us that "my thoughts are not your thoughts, neither are your ways my ways" (Isa. 55:8). There we have it: a verse we all know but usually ignore. When we take time to find out what God wants in each circumstance, we'll discover that He is full of variation. One never knows what He will decide to do next.

We can become so engrained in what has worked in the past that we make our habits into a structure, thinking it always has to be done a particular way. We assume we have "got it down now," similar to Moses striking the rock again instead of speaking to it as God asked the second time around (Num. 26:2–13).

Just as Moses and the Israelites who were saved out of Egypt didn't enter God's rest because they didn't listen to Him, so we can miss God's best because of unbelief, disobedience, and lack of faith (Heb. 3:16–19). God wants us to do His work, His way . . . and to believe that it will work and that it will be the correct thing.

His ways are right, sufficient, and perfect. We need to give Him the space to be the holy God that He is and to make the choices for us.

The church today is busy. The body is scattered. Ministers are trying to do what they think will draw people in. However, God doesn't ask us to devise our own ways and then set out to accomplish them for Him. He simply invites us to get into the coracle with Him and hold on tight. Come on! Let's catch the wind!

THINGS TO CONSIDER . . .

1. The author states that the Celtic church probably would have viewed the church today as being rather boring and unadventurous. Do you agree with such an assessment of our contemporary church? Why or why not?

2. What examples do you know of where the church today has been as courageous and adventurous as the monks setting out in their coracle without an oar?

3. Is there a difference between discovery and gimmicks or trying new methods? Explain your answer.

4. Do you think you could find twelve people from your church to live on Skellig Michael and pray for a lifetime? Why or why not?

5. In your estimation, is the church on the move today? Support your answer.

6. What is the difference between being busy and being on the move by the Holy Spirit?

7. The poem "Little Gidding" by T. S. Elliot has an interesting message:

> We shall not cease from exploration
>
> and the end of all our exploring
>
> will be to arrive where we started
>
> and know the place for the first time.

How does this poem relate to you personally?

8. Where are you at in regards to your devotional life and prayer, that special connecting with God? Is it vibrant? Nonexistent? Something to check off your to-do list?

9. The author says that Jesus "was and is cross-cultural, counter-cultural, and surprising." How have you seen this in action? Is this your view of Him? What Scriptures support these ideas?

Chapter Two

JESUS GIVES GIFTS TO THE CHURCH

Ephesians 4 is worth a few minutes of study since it is the backdrop for this entire book. This passage begins with a clear call to unity in verses 1–6. In the midst of a fragmented and argumentative world, Christians are asked to live worthy lives and to maintain the unity that comes from God alone: The church is called upon to remember what it can agree upon and to keep the "bond of peace." How appealing such a church is to the world!

GRACE

Paul goes on in Ephesians 4:7–10 to say this:

> But to each one of us grace has been given as Christ apportioned it. This is why it says: "When he ascended on high, he took many captives and gave gifts to his people." (What does "he ascended" mean except that he also descended to the lower, earthly regions? He who descended is the very one who ascended higher than all of the heavens in order to fill the whole universe.)

> *The main purpose of the five ministry gifts is to prepare God's people for the work of the ministry.*

Paul shifts from all of us being united together in the body of Christ to address us as individuals: "each of us." The church will never be revitalized without individuals being revitalized. If we want to have a strong and healthy church, we aren't dealing with an amorphous mass or a team of pastors and a board of deacons. Rather, *each member of the body* has to exhibit godly characteristics in order to have a shift in the church.

Thankfully, God makes His resources available to each person in order to build a strong body. Christ apportions grace individually—"to each of us." No one is left out. Each Christian is given enough of this wonderful provision of grace to successfully carry out their particular function in the body of Christ. Whatever area of ministry and contribution we've been designed to do, God provides enough for us to fulfill it.

Paul goes on to refer to Jesus descending into the grave and winning the victory over hell, Satan, and death. Jesus then arose victorious and ascended into heaven, leading a train of captives. This is an amazing picture of the way the ancient world celebrated victories, and it helps us understand Paul's point here.

When a Roman general returned from many months of battle, he formed a victory parade that passed through the Triumphal Gate on a prescribed course of nearly four kilometers through the streets of Rome. The march began with the foreign captives. Those of high status were put on display behind bars and hauled through the streets on wagons, while the captured armies walked along in degradation and chains. These included types of people the average Roman had never seen, with different colors of hair and skin and unusual features. Thousands of Roman citizens lined the streets to see this spectacle.

Next came a display of the weapons and armor the Roman soldiers had captured, along with gold and silver, statuary, and exotic treasures. Paintings and models depicted significant episodes of the war. All the senators and magistrates walked next in line, dressed in prestigious garb.

The general himself came next, riding in a decorated carriage pulled by four horses. He wore a crown of laurel on his head and sported a purple toga with gold embroidery. He was touted with music and pomp. His generals marched with him in red robes, and his other officers surrounded him on horseback. Then came all the Roman legions, unarmed. The horses were carefully groomed and decorated with braided tails and plumes. Additionally, the booty that had been collected in the war was heaped on wagons and displayed in the parade along with exotic animals like elephants and tigers. The parade could take three days.

Throughout the time of festivity, there were games, entertainment, and elaborate banquets. When the celebration was over, the general divided up the treasure and doled out money to those who had served well. The gifts were extremely generous, making many instantly wealthy.

When Paul referred to Jesus ascending on high, leading captives in His train, and giving gifts to men, he was clearly referring to such a victory parade. The captives were the ones who had held humanity captive in sin. Jesus, however, conquered everything (Satan, hell, death, sin) that had enslaved us. He took those who had been the captors and made them captives, leading them in a train, on display. What a sight!

The wonderful Jesus—whom Satan was sure he had conquered on the cross—instead was resurrected and ascended in triumph into heaven to fill the whole universe. In order to be even more magnanimous, Jesus doles out gifts. He not only gives grace to each believer, but He also provides five leadership gifts to the church.

GIFTS FOR THE CHURCH

Jesus is the one who gives the gifts to the church: apostles, prophets, evangelists, pastors, and teachers. After paying the price to win such a great victory, think of His joy in doling out such presents!

> So Christ himself gave the apostles, the prophets, the evangelists, the pastors and teachers, to equip his people for works of service, so that the body of Christ may be built up until we all reach unity in the faith and in the knowledge of the Son of God and become mature, attaining to the whole measure of the fullness of Christ. (Eph. 4:11–13)

Certainly He considered these gifts to be valuable. He chose them as fitting presents to celebrate His magnificent victory over Satan. Since Jesus is so generous, we dare not neglect any of His precious gifts. He considers them all treasure.

The main purpose of the five ministry gifts is to prepare God's people for the work of the ministry. Several misconceptions are floating around in the church today that lead to the wrong idea of ministry. One is that the ministry is for paid clergy to do. "We have pastors and they are paid to do the ministry" is a rather popular notion, although it's a misunderstanding arising out of church tradition.

In actuality, everyone in the church body is supposed to do the work of the ministry. This is what Ephesians clearly indicates. The main task of the five gifts Jesus bestowed upon the church (apostle, prophet, evangelist, pastor, and teacher) is to equip each person in the body of Christ to minister somewhere within the five ministry currents as God directs. Any church that expects its clergy to do all of the work is sadly in error. Furthermore, clergy who aren't training people to do that work are also missing the most important part of their job.

Jesus gave some to be in each role. He "gave" rather than "set" or "appointed" or "elected" or "passed on the office." He designed and chose these gifts, and He saw them as the means for people to bless the church and help it become all that God intended.

No one role is everything. The roles are to be divided and shared. Because God has determined this generous allocation, there's no reason for elitism or jealousy. All five are meant to focus upon different things and to work together for the fullness of the church.

Not only is one role not meant to take over all the other roles, but not everyone in the body of Christ has been "given" these five roles. Not all are called to the oversight roles. However, I believe more have been given these roles than we presently realize. Some of these aren't full-time or paid church clergy but are still a gift from God to help the currents flow.

According to Paul, the purpose of the full working of all the gifts of leadership is that the church will be built up. If the church isn't growing in numbers or maturity, the neglect of these five gifts is likely to be one of the main reasons. Through the activation of these gifts, we reach the "unity of the Spirit." Evangelists, pastors, teachers, and apostolic and prophetic servants are meant to work together smoothly so the church functions in unity. They are good role models of humility and respect.

Another important outcome when the gifts are all functioning strongly, according to Ephesians, is that the church will come to the knowledge of God. This is no small feat. When we work together, we share various aspects of who God is. There is a broader understanding, a more complete picture of Him. Each one of the "gifts" has a different aspect to focus upon, a special current to oversee with a unique emphasis and a distinctive viewpoint. Together they comprise God's concerns for a healthy church—alone, each is only a portion of what He intends.

The final outgrowth of the five leadership gifts being in full operation is that the church will become mature and attain to the whole measure of the fullness of Christ. The church isn't meant to be a little bit like Jesus but "the whole measure." In short, the church is designed to be alive and robust, mature and whole.

THINGS TO CONSIDER...

1. Do you think the church is properly unified today? What unity do we see in individual church bodies? Denominations? The church as a whole?

2. Here is a quote from chapter two: "The main task of the five gifts Jesus bestowed upon the church (apostle, prophet, evangelist, pastor, and teacher) is to equip each person in the body of Christ to minister somewhere within the five ministry currents as God directs." Do you think this is possible in this day and age? How have you seen this in action?

3. Do you believe we are using all five of the ministry gifts in the church today? Explain your answer.

4. Are Christians in general aware that they are supposed to "do the work of the ministry" (Eph. 4:12)? Are they being prepared to do these "works of service"?

5. The outgrowth of training people to do the work of the ministry is that "the church is mature, attaining to the whole measure of the fullness of Christ" (Eph. 4:13). If we were to compare the church to the lifespan of a woman, where would it be on the maturity level? Is the church a mature woman ready to be a bride?

6. Considering that Jesus gave the five ministry gifts as magnificent awards for His great victory over Satan and sin, do you think we value these precious presents as much as we should?

Chapter Three

THE POWERFUL WOOING CURRENT

The heart of God yearns for all people to come into right relationship with Him. He woos us to Himself. Thankfully He doesn't pound us to smithereens but instead, tries not to break the bruised reed or snuff out the smoldering wick (Isa. 42:3). He desires to heal our hurts, transform our lives, save our souls, forgive our transgressions, and make us into new people with a future. All members of the Trinity have the same heart in this matter.

We can see the Father's care in John 3:16, indicating that He loves the world so much He was willing to send His only Son so that we might have eternal life.

One of the main tasks of the Holy Spirit is to "convict the world of sin, and of righteousness, and of judgment" (John 16:8–9, NKJV). We don't have to do the convicting; that's the role of the Holy Spirit. In our society it's sometimes difficult to explain sin to people in ways they will hear. Folks often feel they can do whatever is right in their own eyes. The Holy Spirit, however, can accomplish this work so they will turn to the Savior.

Paul, Silas, and Timothy, in their letter to the Thessalonians, said it was clear the church people there were chosen by God because their sharing of the gospel came "not simply with

> *If God isn't in charge of what we say and do, we might as well not bother.*

words, but also with power, with the Holy Spirit and deep conviction" (1 Thess. 1:5). D. L. Moody once said, "There is not a better evangelist in the world than the Holy Spirit."

Jesus likewise came to seek and to save the lost. He says in John 4:35 that we should not say, "There are still four months more and then comes the harvest" (NKJV). Unfortunately, we often think this way. We believe that someday in the future people will get swept into the kingdom. Jesus corrects this thought. "Open your eyes and look at the fields! They are ripe for harvest. Even now the one who reaps draws a wage and harvests a crop for eternal life, so that the sower and the reaper may be glad together" (vv. 35–36).

The last thing Jesus said before His ascension was this: "But you will receive power when the Holy Spirit comes on you; and you will be my witnesses in Jerusalem, and in all Judea and Samaria, and to the ends of the earth" (Acts 1:8). Similarly Matthew 28:19 states, "Therefore go and make disciples of all nations." Although we have preached and taught much about this commission, the church hasn't followed it particularly well.

Note that Jesus used the word go. Go means "go out." However, the church today tends to say, "Come in." The last I knew, "out" is the opposite of "in." We advertise, hoping people will attend a special event or service. "Come on in and join us," we entreat.

Then we wonder why this doesn't work as well as we hoped. Perhaps it's because Christ expects us to spread the gospel "out there." Before we do, however, He instructs us to wait so we can be empowered to speak effectively and be sensitive to what the

Holy Spirit wants to do and how. Christ doesn't simply give us a commission; He wants to empower us to fulfill that commission.

WAITING

Just before the Lord ascended, He made it clear that He was excited about sending the Holy Spirit. One of the last instructions He gave His disciples was to wait in Jerusalem until they received power from on high (Luke 24:49). Missional evangelism is empowered by waiting first on the Lord. This ministry current doesn't go anywhere without that crucial first step. In reality, no highly effective means of drawing people exist without the Holy Spirit.

Today we aren't inclined to wait. We like fast food, the fast checkout at the supermarket, the fast lane on the highway, and fast service in the restaurant and post office. Waiting seems to be an insult. We have better things to do with our time. Perhaps this attitude explains why we don't see much waiting in church these days. Prayer meetings are sparse. Evening services—where praying at the altars and waiting on God used to be the norm—are no longer in vogue. Most people in a church today don't know what a "tarrying service" or "praying through" even mean.

What does it mean to tarry? We come to God without presenting Him with a list of "to do's." Our watch doesn't get our constant attention. We have no agenda, and we don't allow distractions. Music can sometimes be a diversion and distractor so we may go without it, content to be in the presence of the Lord. We listen carefully, allow His "still, small voice" to speak to us, and let Him get to us. He may rearrange our attitudes, convict, bring us to repentance, change our hearts, strengthen us, prepare us for what is to come, give us an assignment, bring somebody else to mind, provide directions, or pour out an enabling. But none of these things will happen if we don't place ourselves in the waiting mode.

ARE WE BLOCKING THE EFFECTIVENESS OF GOD'S WOOING HEART?

Are we taking enough time to woo the lost these days? Surely this isn't simply about programs, or lights and sound and technology, or fabulous music and good gimmicks. When a young man woos a girl, he's charming and alluring, demonstrating in a thousand little ways that he's desirous of a relationship. He wants to please and win her. He simply wants to be himself, and he hopes she'll like him just as he is.

So it is with the Spirit of God. He woos us, and then He escorts us directly to Jesus Christ. The Spirit wants to introduce us to the incarnate Son of God and invite us to respond. Why is there a response problem these days when God's heart is so desirous of bringing people to Himself? Something must be blocking His desire to have people come into right relationship with Him.

The church in America today is having a hard time. Eighty percent of the churches aren't growing (defined as just 5 percent growth per year). An average of eight churches in the US and Canada close every day.[7] More than half of all churches in America didn't add one new member as measured in 2010–12. Nearly three million previous churchgoers enter the ranks of the "religiously unaffiliated" every single year.[8]

Yes, there have been some strides, but we aren't keeping up, let alone getting ahead. Pew Charitable Trust states, "The number of Christians around the world has nearly quadrupled in 100 years, from about 600 million in 1910 to more than 2 billion in 2010. But the world's overall population also has risen from an estimated 1.8 billion in 1910 to 6.9 billion in 2010."[9] Christians today make up about 32 percent of the world's population as opposed to 35 percent in 1910.

We are in need. This wooing current is not flowing as freely as it should through the church. We tend to wonder what's wrong with those who won't respond, but could the block be us? We've looked to fix this and that, but usually we're looking at programs, buildings, services, and music. Do we possibly think this will accomplish the work of the Spirit?

Jesus stated that when He is "lifted up from the earth," He will "draw all people" to Himself (John 12:32). We should be concerned whether Jesus has the chance to draw people to Himself today. Are we making space in our church mission statements, values, sacraments, and church services, and in our individual lives for Jesus to do this? Are we giving Him the space? Is He being lifted up or are we lifting up our slick ideas and well-done media instead?

Jesus wants to show Himself real and strong. He longs to fill our churches with His presence. He wants to woo, to be tender and loving, healing and forgiving. We can take His presence to work and to our neighborhoods, to the store and the restaurant. As we go out, He will reveal Himself in us if His presence is vibrant and alive in us because we've been waiting on Him.

If God isn't in charge of what we say and do, we might as well not bother. He ought to be front and center, and we should learn to wait and seek His face until He's ready to move. When He does act, the results will be tremendous!

THE DAY OF PENTECOST

The last instructions of our Lord were certainly definitive. He said, "Stay in the city until you have been clothed with power from on high" (Luke 24:49). Just because we aren't used to waiting or don't want to wait doesn't mean this isn't the way to allow the current of God's wooing heart to flow effectively again.

Considering the impetuous nature of Peter, for example, the command to wait couldn't have been easy for him. I've always pictured him as being rather impatient while he waited around the ten days from the ascension until Pentecost. Jesus had shown Himself on earth until His ascension forty days after His resurrection. Now He was gone, and His disciples had seen Him taken into heaven. They knew for sure He was the Son of God, and they surely wanted to tell everybody—but He had told them to *wait*.

Even ten hours would be quite a prayer meeting in this day and age, but that one lasted ten days! They had to sit there, pace, pray, think, pray some more, sit some more, walk around, linger, and then wait some more. Nothing was sure. When would this promised power come? What form would it take? No one knew the answers. So they waited.

How would they know the promised power had arrived? They weren't clear about this either. Perhaps someone like Peter made a little speech like this: "We were told to stay in the city and wait until we received power from on high. I feel powerful; how about you?"

Then maybe a couple of others persuaded him that nothing different had happened, so they all went back to the work of waiting. Yes, the *work*, for that is what it is. Perhaps a few hours later Peter or someone else brought up the topic again. "But think about the fact that we have the good news! God will help us. We should go and share it."

The problem with much of the church today is that it's doing just this. It's trying to share the gospel message in its own strength. Even when the church is going out, it hasn't done the waiting required to empower the message. Though the good news is shared, it lacks the necessary power to impact those who hear. God must be behind it. He is the One—the only One—who activates and energizes the wooing current. It's the difference between reading a love letter and hearing the words directly from the lips of the lover. People today need to hear the living Word from the lips of the One who is saying it to them directly and afresh.

The Scottish evangelist Robert Morrison, who was the first Christian Protestant missionary in China, was asked, "Now Mr.

> *God still wants to empower His people to share the good news effectively with each individual.*

Morrison, do you really expect that you will make an impression on the idolatry of the Chinese Empire?"

He answered, "No, sir, but I expect God will."[10]

Indeed, we need to believe that God is the One who will succeed in evangelism. He has plans and methods beyond our thinking and design. Certainly He acts "outside of the box."

On the day of Pentecost, after waiting so long for God to move, something extraordinary occurred. The day of the baptism in the Holy Spirit was so orchestrated by God that there was an immediate and large audience from everywhere who had gathered in Jerusalem for the Feast of Pentecost (*Shavu'ot*). Because the disciples were now speaking in other tongues, people from numerous tribes and countries (Acts 2:9–11) who had gathered to celebrate the feast could hear in their own language the news that Jesus Christ was the Son of God and had risen from the dead. The result was that they were "amazed and perplexed" and "asked one another, 'What does this mean?'" (Acts 2:12). Because the disciples waited, God orchestrated a surprise that had everybody talking. They were engaged enough to listen. God had their undivided attention!

SPEAKING THE RIGHT LANGUAGE

People still need to hear the good news in their own tongue, whether it be a foreign language or various dialects of the same language. Language embodies how we think and perceive. People should hear about Jesus not only in their native tongue, so they can understand, but also in ways that will affect them with their unique personalities, ages, backgrounds, and cultural perspectives. God still wants to empower His people to share the good news effectively with each individual. He's determined to be personal. He wants to capture every heart's devotion.

God's wooing is effective as He guides us in our communication. He'll nudge us to use certain words and stories if we're sensitive to the Spirit. Perhaps our normal Christian language means nothing to nonbelievers. God knows how to speak with them in ways they'll understand. This means we have to work hard to communicate to each person and cultural group. We need to think about what to say and how to say it. We should practice sometimes and "test out" new ways of expression. This means risk, relinquishing our lingo, and learning to let God express Himself through us in ways presently unfamiliar to us.

We also need to get to know the people with whom we communicate. What is their language exactly? I'm not talking about whether they speak English or Cantonese or Spanish or Swahili. I'm asking what words within each language will best communicate to their hearts. What words might be "loaded" because of bad experiences? What are their biases and their histories? What are their hopes and dreams and motivations? What will turn them off? What will get them excited? What will open them up? What questions will get them talking so we can listen carefully? Consideration of these concerns will prepare the way for God's wooing current to flow.

Our own efforts are useful, but surely they aren't enough. We need to let the Holy Spirit teach us to listen to His inner impulses so we can hear what He wants to say rather than speaking out of our own need to be heard, to feel self-important, or to share only what we already know rather than providing fresh insight. What matters more than anything is what God's Spirit has directed and empowered us to speak at any given moment.

POWER AND BOLDNESS

Billy Graham once said, "I have had the privilege of preaching the gospel on every continent in most of the countries of the world. And I have found that when I present the simple message of the gospel of Jesus Christ, with authority and simplicity and quoting from the very word of God—He takes the message and drives it supernaturally into the human heart. . . . It is a supernatural message, a supernatural authority, a supernatural power, the power of the Holy Spirit."[11]

How do we know if we have this power? Note that in the earlier verse we considered (Luke 24:49) the disciples were told to wait in the city until they were clothed with power from on high. "To put clothes or apparel on someone" is the literal meaning of this word clothed (*enduo*) in the Greek. Some have viewed this as an internal endowment. However, Jesus clearly is using a word to indicate something external, i.e., clothing. When we have this power that God wishes to bestow, it's apparent to others. It doesn't consist of just inward and private traits. What we receive from the Holy Spirit is substantially different from a mere mental shift, a cognitive focus, or an emotional centering. The power is obvious to all.

We do, in fact, know when we are clothed and when we are not. So does everybody else! The power that God wants to give the church for witness, testimony, and effective evangelism is something external and obvious to everybody.

After being threatened by the chief priests and elders and subsequently being released from prison, Peter and John and the other believers prayed an amazing prayer. "Now, Lord, consider their threats and enable your servants to speak your word with great boldness. Stretch out your hand to heal and perform signs and wonders through the name of your holy servant Jesus" (Acts.4:29–30). Verse 31 tells us that after they prayed, "the place where they were meeting was shaken. And they were all filled

> *God's boldness emanates naturally from waiting on God and not trying to do these things in our own abilities.*

with the Holy Spirit and spoke the word of God boldly."

The context for this story teaches us a great deal. Acts 3 (occurring shortly after the day of Pentecost) tells how Peter and John were going to the temple and in the process stopped to speak to a crippled beggar whom God subsequently healed. They began sharing the good news and many believed. For this they were called before the Sanhedrin and drilled. The political scene was sticky, but it resulted in the Sanhedrin letting Peter and John go, after commanding them not to speak or teach at all in the name of Jesus. The answer the disciples gave to this command is telling.

"But Peter and John replied, 'Which is right in God's eyes: to listen to you, or to him? You be the judges! As for us, we cannot help speaking about what we have seen and heard'" (Acts 4:19–20). This is quite an in-your-face comment. They might have said, "Well, we'll try." But instead they basically said they didn't want to follow that command. Furthermore, they *couldn't* follow that command.

I can picture Peter and John throwing up their hands, shrugging their shoulders, raising their eyebrows, and, with their heads cocked a little to the side, saying, "We can't help it!" So true! They couldn't help it. They were set on fire by God. They had waited for the Holy Spirit's empowerment, and they were clothed with power and boldness, and everybody knew it. They had to speak out and share what they knew. They simply couldn't help it!

When they were released, they joined the other believers and prayed for more boldness. They didn't want to be stopped or to have a subtle fear hold them back.

Indeed, boldness is not synonymous with stubborn loudness and insistence. This can be a turnoff. Rather, it's a God-ordained flow and anointing that draws and wins people. We need divinely-imparted power rather than self-generated assertiveness. God's boldness emanates naturally from waiting on God and not trying to do these things in our own abilities. With God's power and strength we won't shrink back but will boldly share what the Spirit desires . . . just that . . . no more and no less. How we need this current flowing again in our time!

GOD'S POWERFUL WOOING CURRENT TODAY

In order for this strong evangelistic stream to return to the church, we need to follow the biblical model. We must wait until we've been clothed with power from on high. We should give ourselves to prayer whenever societal pressure pushes us to become wimps instead of Christian communicators. We need to ask for boldness and let ourselves be shaken up with it so that we, too, can say, "I can't help it," with smiles on our faces and love in our hearts. God is still desirous of getting the lost saved!

Notice that on the day of Pentecost, after they had been baptized in the Holy Spirit, something wonderful happened. Scripture tells us that Peter stood up and preached a sermon, and the people were "cut to the heart" and asked what they should do (Acts 2:37). Peter answered that they should "repent and be baptized, every one of you, in the name of Jesus Christ for the forgiveness of your sins. And you will receive the gift of the Holy Spirit. The promise is for you and your children and for all who are far off—for all whom the Lord our God will call" (Acts 2:38–39).

Peter knew that people would get saved, and about 3,000 were baptized and added to their number that day. What an amazing baptismal service that must have been. Think of it. They went from 120 waiting together in unity in the upper room (waiting, praying, and waiting some more), and suddenly in just a few short hours the Holy Spirit moved, doing the work of God in the hearts of this brand new church. They went out and shortly had 3,120 plus the other disciples who weren't in the upper room.

Hmmm. What about them? Were there more followers? Probably. There may well have been some who didn't wait. Imagine having to tell your grandkids, "I could have been there but I wasn't. I got impatient. I thought I didn't need to wait. I missed the day of Pentecost!"

The Spirit, then and now, comes to those who pray and wait. He teaches and changes us. He prepares us and gives us insight on what He wants to say to people's hearts. He is the wooer, the changer, the transformer, the One who convicts, and He who draws everyone to the Savior. He wants to do an incredible work today.

THINGS TO CONSIDER . . .

1. Jesus said to "go into all the world." What do you think? Is the church today (not just missionaries but the church as a whole) actually going out? Or, as the author suggests, is the church more likely to invite people to come in? How, exactly, could we do a better job of going out?

2. Do you think that the church today relies enough on the Holy Spirit to convict people of sin? If people aren't being convicted, why might that be?

3. "Missional evangelism is empowered by waiting first on the Lord." Why should we wait on the Lord and not just go out there and start telling people about Jesus? What difference does it make whether we wait or not?

4. Are our services in the United States too structured? How do we learn to actually spend time waiting on God in a service and individually?

5. How do we go about lifting Jesus up in our church services rather than ourselves, or our media, or any other thing or method?

6. Jesus explained that He only said what His Father wanted Him to say. How can we get closer to being like this?

7. Since boldness is not synonymous with stubborn loudness and insistence, how do we find and release the true boldness of the Holy Spirit? What does the baptism in the Holy Spirit have to do with this boldness?

8. In Luke 24:49 the disciples were told to wait in the city until they were clothed with power from on high. Are we trying to do evangelism on our own, or are we waiting on the Holy Spirit to do His work through us?

Chapter Four

THE EVANGELIST

Our concept of an evangelist today is perhaps reserved for several particular types. These are full-time workers who are well-known, hold large meetings, often in different countries, where many thousands of people come to Christ. In this group we would place people from the last 150 years like Billy Graham, John Whitefield, Aimee Semple McPherson, Billy Sunday, Dwight L. Moody, Kathryn Kuhlman, Charles Finney, Charles Spurgeon, Maria Woodworth-Etter, Duncan Campbell, Steve Hill, and Carlos Annacondia. Certainly the list is longer and goes back further into history.

We would probably also look to those people who travel from church to church and hold "evangelistic services." These special meetings are often held for several nights in a row with an emphasis on bringing in friends to hear the good news.

Unfortunately, the word *evangelist* has often taken on a negative connotation in our postmodern society. Movies have characterized the evangelist as a hypocritical, red-faced, spitting, shouting personage who is more concerned with numbers than with individuals. The world's concept often includes someone who tries to coerce others through whatever means possible to come over to their own way of thinking. Non-Christians consider pressure and strong-arm tactics to be the norm. Even in a nicer light, evangelists are often considered to be zealous advocates who have a high level of enthusiasm and are determined to have people change at almost any cost.

God loves people and wants to see them drawn to Him. We don't need to pound and yell loudly in order to convince them. Richard C. Halverson, chaplain of the United States Senate for more than a decade, made a great comment. He said, "Evangelism is not salesmanship. It is not urging people, pressing them, coercing them, overwhelming them, or subduing them. Evangelism is telling a message. Evangelism is reporting good news."[12]

HOW THE EVANGELIST AFFECTS THE LOCAL CHURCH

People who are called out by God and anointed to lead His powerful wooing current of evangelism must let Him share His extravagant love through them. Those who are called to this role will have a deep compassion for people regardless of age, outward appearance, cultural background, or sin propensity. They'll be concerned with individuals and their personal needs.

Evangelists care just as much about a waitress or taxi cab driver or corporate executive as they do about a big event with hundreds in attendance. They value these equally and give their all in every circumstance. This was true of Jesus. He took time to minister to individuals and small groups as readily as to crowds. Size didn't matter to Him. What mattered were the people God brought into His path and the state of their hearts.

With this is mind, our concept of the evangelist as an event-oriented individual or traveling speaker is skewed. These people are indeed part of what God wants to do, but they're not the whole picture. The Lord wants all of His disciples—every single one of them—to reach out to the lost and make a difference.

God has entrusted all believers with the ministry of reconciliation (2 Cor. 5:18–19). We need the evangelistic leadership in our churches to train *everybody* to share this message well.

The local evangelists need to stir up love and concern for all kinds of individuals. They should help church people learn how to pray and intercede for others. They can show people how to wait in God's presence where they'll be empowered to do and say what He wants. And finally, they can model what God-generated evangelism looks like.

Without this kind of modeling, people will try to do what God commands without the power of the Holy Spirit. It's a sad picture when this happens. "Too many Christians are no longer fishers of men but keepers of the aquarium," quipped Paul Harvey. Certainly the local evangelists need to teach others how to fish, not just hound them to do it, but the Holy Spirit provides the hook.

EVANGELISTIC LEADERS ABOUND

People who could potentially have a gifting for evangelistic leadership are all around us. God has called many, though some aren't aware of their own calling since they think evangelists are only of the big-event or traveling variety. Nonetheless, God has given them all similar traits that can easily be observed.

I have a friend who is a big-event evangelist. He's outgoing, friendly, and sometimes a little overwhelming. He can talk to anybody. I'm not exactly a shrinking wallflower, but next to him I feel like one. He's always out there with something to say, and he can strike up a conversation anywhere and people start talking about their private problems. Once I was having lunch with him and his wife. I noticed our table didn't have any pepper so I reached to get it from a table behind me. When I turned around again, he had led our waitress to the Lord. Of course, I'm using a bit of hyperbole here. But, really, he was just chatting with her and by the time I turned around he was praying with her.

Another friend is a school administrator who also has the gift of evangelism. He's won so many people to the Lord and also has trained his students to share the good news. These in turn have gone out all over their country winning people to Christ on buses, in the train stations where homeless people hang out, in the parks, on street corners, everywhere! I could tell story after story because I've heard their testimonies. This is so encouraging!

When the evangelistic gifting is flowing, others get excited that they can do it too. It's modeled for them by the leader. Even going out two-by-two—which was the way Jesus sent out His disciples—can help others as they watch, pray, and participate as the Spirit leads.

I believe our churches are blessed with people who have evangelistic giftings of various kinds. Look around. It could be that friendly usher or the deacon who doesn't know a stranger. It might be the greeter at the door or the person who invites all their friends to church, where they get saved.

Although there are what I have called big-event and travelling evangelists, many other people with this gifting are called to stay close to the local church. They care about individuals and want to impact them. They open the doors into the church community. Some are good at inviting people to events and helping ease them into new circumstances. Others talk easily with new acquaintances and shape the gospel message around people's interests. Many are good at persuading, mentoring, and walking with people until they're ready to make a decision for Christ. They model Jesus through their living and are winsome. The local evangelists are attractional, even magnetic.

With this broader and more comprehensive view of evangelists, it's easy to see how many present and potential evangelistic leaders there are in the church. I've seen door greeters who are

> *Those who like to connect with people and move in the gift of hospitality can easily build friendships and are often great evangelists.*

so friendly that people are just drawn to them. Some churches have extra greeters on hand so one who connects with a newcomer can take off and lead the person to their child's Sunday school class or accompany them into the worship service where they can chat and find out more about that person, perhaps networking them with others in their vocation or area of interest.

Those who like to connect with people and move in the gift of hospitality can easily build friendships and are often great evangelists. Some are adept at apologetics in an easygoing way and can clearly answer questions that have bothered folks for years—and do it with a smile and with ease.

All these in the church body are prime candidates to be considered as evangelists. They might not think of themselves as evangelists because they know they aren't Billy Graham. But perhaps we haven't widely understood or affirmed the variety this gifting entails. As we become more observant of Christians and their God-given gifting, we can place these potential evangelists in spots to lead out. With more leaders to precipitate the flow through the Holy Spirit, the powerful wooing current will surge forth more naturally and completely in our churches today. God knows we need it!

TRUE CONVERSIONS

In evangelism, people don't simply want to encounter us acting like Jesus, although this is good. Their greatest desire isn't for

> *When people are radically saved, they will do anything to serve the Lord.*

us to "be Jesus to them," which at best is a shadow of the real thing. What they need most is to encounter Jesus Himself, and certainly He is perfectly capable and desirous of this. In fact, our attempts can't substitute for this living encounter.

The hearts of those who have yet to be saved are longing for Jesus. They might not know it yet, but that's exactly and only what they want. If we haven't lingered in His presence, we can't bring His presence to those who need it. It's impossible to take people where we haven't gone.

When we don't spend time with God first, we have little to give the lost. We can offer pressure and nervousness . . . a verse . . . some words of our own. But the Bible verses have to come alive through Jesus, the living Word! The Spirit has to do the work of conviction and persuasion. In so many ways this is a relief. We don't have to figure it all out. But we do have to wait on God so He can move through us and touch each person in the way He desires.

An example of this occurred when revival came in 1948 to the Island of Harris and Lewis in the Scottish Hebrides where Duncan Campbell was preaching. In his little booklet called *The Nature of a God-Sent Revival*, Campbell talks about a young lady, a nurse in Glasgow, who was in terrible distress of soul for a long period of time. Her father thought perhaps Campbell could assist her, and he agreed to visit. He knelt beside her and shared a Scripture verse with her (John 10:27) and tried to provide some words that would help her. The answer she gave him through her tears is striking: "Mr. Campbell, I thank you for your kindly words of counsel, but surely, surely, as a minister, you believe that a verse of Scripture won't save you?"[13]

We have to let God do the work of wooing and saving a person. We can't lead them so quickly to a simple and quick prayer at an altar that they aren't brought through by the power of God into a renewed life. Some sitting in our church pews have such "shallow conversions" that they've never understood the depth of their sin and the amazing work Jesus accomplished in forgiving them and setting them free. They haven't truly converted, which literally means "turn from." They think they can keep their sin and follow their own ways while adding Jesus into their repertoire. People who become Christians must agree to let Jesus thoroughly save them from their sins and commit to Him all the way.

I've heard an altar call given which was pretty much saying, "Accept Jesus and He will make you happy. It's so easy. Just say a little prayer with me." This certainly isn't a true message. Jesus isn't a fast train ticket to heaven or a convenience. Scripture asks us, rather, to die to ourselves and to follow Him. Salvation is free, but it demands everything!

Indeed, the good news must be presented in its completeness and depth. We shouldn't be winning people over to a god who has no demands of obedience or requires nothing from us. Such a god is not the true One. God wants to draw each person to Himself and radically change their lives, but He doesn't allow people to cut corners or to have it their way. He doesn't bargain.

When the Spirit does a deep work of conviction of sin, Jesus profoundly saves, and God graciously accepts that person into His fold for eternity. He wants fruit that remains. That's what happened to the nurse in three or four days after Campbell visited her. She came through to the Lord in great joy; there was a real transformation. When people are radically saved, they will do anything to serve the Lord. He laid down His life for them; they will do the same for Him.

God is already at work in people's lives before salvation. Throughout their journey together, God has allowed spiritual appetites to develop and a hunger to grow that will continue to motivate the new convert to be faithful. The Father instigates and keeps having a divine conversation with them that shouldn't be interrupted by any human, strident voice. God is both the Author and Finisher of our faith. We don't need to hurry out and anxiously clinch the deal on His behalf; we can trust Him to complete the whole work. Yes, He may use us, but He doesn't want us to get in His way!

THE EVANGELIST AS PRAYER LEADER

Surely the evangelist should be able to model what it's like to hear from God—to be receptive to what He wants to say and how He wants to say it. Andrew Murray once mentioned that the person "who mobilizes the Christian church to pray will make the greatest contribution to world evangelization in history." Evangelists should be able to lead people to the altars where they learn to hear from God about their witnessing.

When we believe that God is in charge of the salvation process, it can change the way we intercede for those who don't know Him. We can pray for more of an appetite for God in their lives, rather than ease of life. We can pray for God's timing rather than ours in their salvation process. We may ask that they'll encounter Jesus, for the Holy Spirit to ignite the Word of life, for them to submit to the wooing of Jesus and to sense His love, and for them to meet others who will be living for Jesus in a way that will intrigue them.

The people in the church should stop focusing on themselves and their own guilt for not winning the lost and start focusing instead on the needs of the persons for whom they're praying. Believers can ask that God will position them to be used under His direction and empowered by the Spirit in the waiting/intercession time as

> *Events designed around people look differently than those planned around a program.*

the Lord Himself works to draw others to Himself.

Besides this kind of prayer for individuals, we need to see the even bigger picture. Evangelists should also model how to intercede for a country or a city or a neighborhood. Rather than simply teaching techniques for evangelism, the leaders should also be able to demonstrate how to come into the presence of God and pray for people groups, nations, and religious strongholds. This is perhaps one of the greatest gifts an evangelist can give to the church: the revelation of God's yearning for the lost and a simulation of Jesus interceding.

Surely we can pray for ourselves and those we love, but sometimes we just need to move out! Evangelism is a big picture. God wants to be known in many places. As we bless others and pray for their well-being, our cities and countries can change and provides an atmosphere that is more conducive to people accepting Christ. This is all certainly a critical part of the evangelism current.

LOVING PEOPLE SINCERELY

When we take time to pray to God about those He has placed on our hearts, something happens. We start to love them more, to have compassion and better understanding, and to become more sensitive to their needs and points of view. God teaches us how to *agape* them without an agenda, as opposed to thinking of them as an evangelism project. He gives us patience along with creative ideas about how to be a true friend to them.

Too often we plan church events without people in mind. Oh, we want to see people attend, all right. But we aren't planning the events with the deep needs or true interests of the people in our hearts. As we pray for individuals, God will give an understanding of what might be helpful to them. Events designed around people look differently than those planned around a program.

How easy it is to evaluate an event based upon numbers rather than what happened in peoples' lives. Chuck Miller espouses the latter. In his book *The Spiritual Formation of Leaders*, Miller suggests the importance of developing an expanded set of evaluative criteria. He states:

> We who are in leadership must focus on what is primary: What did God's Spirit do in people's lives? What did His Spirit do in us leaders? We must focus on celebrating the people stories and God's transforming work in their lives. Later, we can evaluate the nuts and bolts of the event—but not for at least a few days. We goal-oriented folks too often rush to evaluation, and, driven by the let's-improve-the-event dynamic, we miss the joy of seeing God touch lives and transform people.[14]

Perhaps this is a great way of determining whether or not we really love people. Are we more concerned with the slickness of the program or with what happened to people? Indeed, it's sometimes difficult to know the answer to this question. But it's exciting to hear feedback and testimonies—not to boost our own egos but to understand how God has been at work in those He loves.

I have a particular pet peeve. It's when people ask me after an event I have ministered at how it went. How do I know the answer to that? Even when it comes to results, how can I tell? Perhaps the altars were full at the end, but does that mean there were any real changes in those people? Maybe they cried and repented, but did they go back to doing the same old thing the next day? Or what if no one came to the altar? Does that mean no one was touched? No, not at all. I've had services where I wondered if anything at all happened of eternal value, but later I've gone back to that same place and someone has come up to me and said, "That service changed my life last year! I haven't been the same since that night." This is the testimony I love to hear.

We should give more time to personal testimonies today. Oh, I understand why they have disappeared. Some people were inclined to talk on and on. Others focused upon themselves instead of God. Many were trivial ("God healed my hangnail!"). But surely people can be taught to take care of these problems.

Furthermore, testimonies might be lacking because we tend to be so self-reliant. We're perhaps not always desperate enough to go to Jesus and have a marvelous testimony as a result of faith. This is to our detriment because we don't see God at work.

In one country I visited, testimonies are given all the time. The pastor asks for people who want to share to come up to the altar. They rush forward and the elders and deacons are there and listen to their report. These leaders choose three or four who will share, giving them instructions. The pastor holds the mike. I still have testimonies that encourage me lodged in my soul from these experiences—testimonies of faith, of God coming through for people, of provision, of transformation, and marvelous salvation.

Those leading the evangelism current should allow for such words of encouragement and demonstrations of faith. They bring people to Jesus by showing that He is alive and active in our world today. Revelation 12:11 states that they overcame him (Satan) "by the blood of the Lamb and by the word of their testimony." Think of putting those two together. The blood of Jesus is most efficacious, so our testimony is incredibly powerful in loosening the hold the Devil has on people's lives.

When we truly love people, we'll be zealous to hear their stories. We'll listen carefully to what they have to say. I've done extensive study in questioning techniques and find that it's an amazing tool for evangelization. Jesus asked questions all the time. They made people think, and usually they had to continue to ponder for a while. But Jesus was never busy formulating His next question rather than listening. He paid attention with His heart, and people knew it and responded in same. This kind of evangelism comes only when we care sincerely for people.

THINGS TO CONSIDER . . .

1. What is your perspective of an evangelist? Where do you think your ideas came from?

2. In the Scottish revival in the Hebrides in 1948, lack of attendance at the prayer meetings was considered sufficient reason to doubt a person's conversion. What would happen if we applied this same measure today in our churches?

3. How can we learn more about going to God in prayer for unbelievers? Do you agree that everyone must be in God's presence before they run out to share the gospel?

4. How do we go about making effective testimony a greater part of our lives and churches?

5. Who do you see in your local church who is part of the evangelistic work?

6. How strong do you think the wooing current is presently in your church? In the church universal? How can we strengthen this current so it flows more freely?

Chapter Five

THE RADICAL FORMING CURRENT

---⚛---

It takes a great deal of effort to help people come to the point of being born again. Then we go through an agonizing process all over again as we work with them until Christ is formed in their lives. If we're part of this discipleship or forming current, we shouldn't be surprised when we face travail, discomfort, and frustration. The forming process takes a while, and there are ups and downs.

This current has crucial aspects. It matures the new believer into Christlikeness. Our term *discipleship* has come to mean different things, but inasmuch as it's effectively teaching people to follow Jesus closely and be His enrolled student, discipleship is also part of the forming current. A disciple is the student of a teacher. The goal of the forming current is to make mature followers of Christ who become like Him.

Paul provided a graphic picture of the forming current in Galatians 4:19 where he stated: "My dear children, for whom I am again in the pains of childbirth until Christ is formed in you." In order for this to occur, we need to sit under a master teacher, and that is the triune God. The master teacher is the One who knows the most, the One who has the final say, the One we would most prefer to teach us. In the case of God, we have the

> *The Holy Spirit knows God and shares with us what God thinks.*

Father, the Son, and the Holy Spirit, all of whom are master teachers and who instruct us in different areas.

Let's begin by considering the Father. In Psalm 32:8 He says, "I will instruct you and teach you in the way which you should go; I will counsel you with my loving eye on you." The Father is certainly in the teaching business. Throughout Scripture we find people saying that they want to meet with God the Father so that He might teach them His ways. He told Moses that He would teach him what he was to do (Ex. 4:15). Job 36:22 states: "God is exalted in his power. Who is a teacher like him?"

Like any good earthly father, our heavenly Father is willing to share His wisdom, views, perspectives, and means so that we can grow into whole people. The world uses information-withholding as a means of power. Our Father, however, demonstrates His inclusive, generous nature by sharing information with us, revealing Himself. He wants to provide a flow of information through His Word so we can grasp the truth and apply it to our lives.

Jesus also was constantly called teacher and rabbi (rabbi being the Hebrew word for "teacher" or "master of the Torah"). In Matthew 7:28–29 the people were amazed at His teaching because He taught as one having authority. Of course He did, because the Father had given that authority to Him and because He spent time in His Father's presence learning what He was to say and do. He taught well because He listened well.

Even when they were trying to trap Him, the Pharisees recognized His teaching was different. "'Teacher,' they said, 'we know that you are a man of integrity and that you teach the way of

God in accordance with the truth. You aren't swayed by others, because you pay no attention to who they are'" (Matt. 22:16).

God wants a strong forming current in the church that flows with instruction directly from His throne. It entails His words, His directions and ways, His correction and warnings, His admonitions and encouragement. God conceives of this current as truly radical because it emanates from Him. The term *radical* has at times come to mean out there on the edge or extreme. The origin of the word, however, is from the Latin word *radix*, which means "root." The strong forming current in the church should be designed to keep the Christian faith rooted in the truth, which in and of itself will shake up the world.

Jesus constantly tapped into this current and shared precisely what God the Father wanted Him to speak. He declared, "My teaching is not my own. It comes from the one who sent me" (John 7:16). This comment is Jesus' answer to those who were amazed and asked how Jesus could have gained such learning. His answer is so important. He wasn't sharing ideas from other people; He was sharing truth from God. What a vast difference exists between these two kinds of teaching!

Today the church needs to have people walk away from their teaching/learning opportunities saying, "That was amazing!" We should value this as much as we value good comments about our worship, programs, or sermons. When the teaching current is flowing directly from God's throne room, people will be changed and will grow into what He intends for them. They'll develop fully and become mature.

How interesting to note that in the New Testament alone, "teaching" is mentioned seventy-four times, "teach" forty-five times, "teacher" fifty-two times, and "Rabbi" sixteen times. The term "disciple" is listed a staggering 269 times! This is contrasted to "preaching," which is mentioned thirty-one times, and "preach" and "preacher," which are mentioned twice each.

I wonder whether we're concerned enough about the teaching aspects of our churches.

The role of the Holy Spirit is to be the Counselor, to teach, to remind people of what has been said from the living Word (John 14:23–26). The Holy Spirit knows God and shares with us what God thinks. We can't do this by ourselves; we need the Spirit. "The Spirit searches all things, even the deep things of God. For who knows a person's thoughts except their own spirit within them? In the same way no one knows the thoughts of God except the Spirit of God" (1 Cor. 2:10–11).

As people who live by the Spirit, we need to grasp the significance of this in fresh ways. The Spirit desires to share with us the mind and heart of God. The Spirit searches it all out! Then He turns around and reveals it to us. Just as our own spirits know what we're thinking—but others can only guess at it—so the Spirit of God knows what God is thinking. He doesn't hide it and make us guess at it but shares with us what He thinks.

Some of the strongest work of the Holy Spirit is related to His being our Counselor, revealing the Father's mind to us and guiding us into all truth. John 16:13 states: "But when he, the Spirit of truth, comes, he will guide you into all truth. He will not speak on his own; he will speak only what he hears, and he will tell you what is yet to come."

Obviously the work of each member of the Trinity is highly related to teaching. Teaching/discipleship is meant to receive substantial value, commitment, and energy from the church, but does it? Do we think about it, pray, pine over it, and concern ourselves, or do we toss it aside as a secondary concern?

Teaching for the Trinity is a primary necessity and so it should be for us. God woos people, but He doesn't intend to leave them alone. Jesus' last great order included both the wooing current and the forming current that teaches maturity and discipleship. In God's master plan for the church, these are vitally integrated.

FORMING DISCIPLES

Unfortunately, the Great Commission is sometimes presented in shorthand. We often get the idea that what it entails is to go and make converts. Notice Matthew 28:18–20:

> Then Jesus came to them and said, "All authority in heaven and on earth has been given to me. Therefore go and make disciples of all nations, baptizing them in the name of the Father and of the Son and of the Holy Spirit, and teaching them to obey everything I have commanded you."

Note that Jesus began the Great Commission by referring to the authority He had been given. He passed on to us the radical enabling required to go and make disciples. We couldn't possibly do it otherwise. We need Him to be with us.

The end process here, however, is not to make converts. It isn't to have people accept Jesus into their lives by saying a prayer. Conversion is a first step, but surely it isn't the final result. Otherwise it would be like having a baby and being satisfied that it stays around eight to ten pounds and never grows or changes. The outcome God has in mind is to bring people to the point of maturity so they become like the Savior.

Part of the maturation process needs to include baptism and all it stands for: dying to the old self and being raised to a transformed life in Jesus. The baptism is into all three members of the Trinity, who have similar aspects and yet a variety of contributions. This doesn't merely entail the naming of each member of the Trinity in a ceremony but a complete immersion into each person of the Triune God and everything they represent and value.

Furthermore, we are to include all nations in the discipleship process. In Christ's Great Commission, there's no arrogance or placing of oneself above others. All are important and desirous to Him in the teaching process.

> *God intends for us to journey alongside those who are saved all the way through to maturity.*

Finally in this passage, Jesus includes teaching again. He puts an almost unbelievable responsibility upon us. He says we are to teach "everything" that He has commanded; we aren't to leave anything out. Furthermore, we aren't simply supposed to tell it but to teach people how to obey it.

What a task! Is it possible, however, that we have conceived of it only partially? Today I believe I hear a lot more about making converts than I do about teaching them. And if I were to consider it further, I think programs are being pushed more than disciple-making.

Dallas Willard, in his book *The Great Omission: Reclaiming Jesus's Essential Teaching on Discipleship*, states the following:

> For those who lead or minister, there are yet graver questions. What authority or basis do I have to baptize people who have not been brought to a clear decision to be a disciple of Christ? Dare I tell people, as "believers" without discipleship, that they are at peace with God and God with them? Where can I find justification for such a message? Perhaps most important: Do I as a minister have the faith to undertake the work of disciple-making? Is my first aim to make disciples? Or do I just run an operation?[15]

God intends for us to journey alongside those who are saved all the way through to maturity. We need to be conscious of where each convert is along the way in their individual growth and development. This is the responsibility of the church. May God help us to serve up meat instead of milk. We shouldn't have to provide games and distractions for mature believers so we can hold their attention. Hopefully we won't have to keep focusing only on the elementary components of the Christian life. God wants His kids to grow up!

BEING A DISCIPLE

Biblical maturation leaves no room for the idea of being converted and choosing not to be a disciple. They go together irretrievably. In fact, we can't really be a Christian without also being a disciple and becoming more like Jesus. The good news of evangelism is shared initially, but then it continues as new believers discover who Jesus is and learn to live out and apply the gospel in their daily lives.

Such ongoing discipleship means that the person doesn't commit to an ideological thought or ticket to a good life but to the person of Jesus. We abandon all else in order to follow along with Him in relationship, just as Jesus' disciples did.

When Jesus called Peter and his brother Andrew to be His disciples, He said, "Come, follow me . . . and I will send you out to fish for people." Scripture tells us that "at once they left their nets and followed him" (Matt. 4:19–20). Becoming a disciple meant dropping everything and following Jesus wherever He went.

Jesus made this perfectly clear in Mark 8:34 when He said, "If anyone would come after me, he must deny himself and take up his cross and follow me." Jesus asked the rich young ruler to go and sell everything and then follow Him. He asks us to let nothing stand between us and Him. Not a single thing or person is more important than He is. We have to follow Him no matter what.

We must make a place for radical commitment to Jesus in our churches today. Instead of saying, "We hope you can find time to spend an hour with us for a little teaching next week," true discipleship calls for a person's entire life to be handed over for the purpose of transformation. Jesus paid it all; we must lay it all down. If this sounds extreme, it is. Nonetheless, it is the true gospel message. The teaching and discipleship current requires us to die to everything so that we might live. God has a good plan for us at the end, but we have to do it His way.

For the radical forming current to flourish and flow as God intends, the church needs many more people who can model what it's like to live sold-out to Jesus Christ as full-fledged disciples who hold back nothing for themselves. We need people who are willing to take up their crosses and die to themselves. This is what it truly means to be a disciple. Our church is in crisis when the majority of people sitting in the pews don't have this view of themselves. They aren't willing to work on behalf of God's kingdom or pull themselves out of their easy chairs and away from their entertainment.

Our present church culture promotes leadership, which has left us in a discipleship crisis. Leaders may be tempted to ask Jesus to bless and follow them and their plans rather than to follow Jesus and His plans. It's a subtle and terrible trap to fall into.

Leonard Sweet says this in his book, *I Am a Follower: The Way, Truth, and Life of Following Jesus*:

Fundamental to biblical faith are two categorical imperatives:

1. Jesus is the Leader.

2. We are his followers.

The Christian life can be succinctly summarized using a child's playground game, "Follow the Leader." That game, if you remember, was more about how to be a follower than it was about being a leader.

In this book, I assign the word Leader to Jesus singly and only. You and I are never leaders, only followers. The best we can aspire to is to become first followers, not followers who then go on to be leaders. We are always followers— followers first and then first followers. Even when we are summoned to the front of the line, we still are behind our Leader.

This is not to say that a follower does not have tremendous influence. Followers often like to follow other followers as much as they like to follow the Leader. By the way we live, we influence others to follow Jesus one way or another. But first followers are always trying to get out of the way and make others first followers of Jesus as well.[16]

The church today needs to be a body of radically-committed followers who are growing in the knowledge of Christ and maturing, becoming more like Him every day. A full flow of the radical forming current in the church requires that every single person including those in charge—take personal discipleship seriously. People in the church long to understand what it means to follow the leadership of Jesus. Only those who are so committed can be teachers who lead out this critical aspect of church health that Jesus commanded: "Go now and make disciples."

THINGS TO CONSIDER . . .

1. Jesus said, "My teaching is not my own. It comes from the one who sent me" (John 7:16). How much teaching are you getting from the Father (including from people who listen to God and share His mind) as opposed to receiving the popular ideas of the world today?

2. The author notes that the words "disciple" and "teaching" (in one form or another) are used much more in scripture than the word "preaching." Is it possible we have been emphasizing preaching too much at the expense of discipleship and teaching?

3. Jesus said to "go and make disciples of all nations . . . teaching them to obey everything I have commanded you" (Matt. 28:19–20). Has the church today read this "go and make converts" instead? Are we really teaching people to obey everything Jesus said?

4. Since the goal is to bring people to be like Jesus, how is this being accomplished in your church? Is it working? Are you yourself being formed into a complete follower of Jesus Christ?

5. The author states the following: "For the radical forming current to flourish and flow as God intends, the church needs many more people who can model what it is like to live sold-out to Jesus Christ as full-fledged disciples who hold back nothing for themselves." How are you living sold-out to Christ? What more could you do for Him. How about your church?

6. In what ways has your church demonstrated its commitment to Christian education?

7. What does a fully formed disciple of Christ look like?

Chapter Six

THE TEACHER

When we step onto the path of following Jesus, He becomes our friend and interacts with us as we spend time in His presence. The life of the Spirit changes us into His likeness. This interaction is vital, real, and completely life-changing. He transforms our thinking, heals our hurts, makes us feel safe and secure, allows us to be ourselves, deals with those actions and thoughts that are hindering us from fullness of life, enables us to obey Him, forgives and accepts, loves and encourages. This is the most wonderful, essential and life-changing relationship we will ever have. If we don't lead people into this relationship and encourage them to maintain it, the loss is incomprehensible.

Dallas Willard said, "Christian spiritual formation is simply indispensable. The lack of an understanding and implementation of it is why there is in general so little real difference between professing Christian and non-Christian today. Where can one find today any real group of Christians with an actual plan to teach the people of their group to do everything Jesus said?"[17]

Teaching people to obey everything Jesus commanded (Matt. 28:20) is part of the Great Commission and is as essential to the life and vitality of the church as evangelism. It demands our attention. Jesus not only interacts with people in discipleship, but He uses people in the process. He wants teachers who are so much like Him that He can entrust others into their care—teachers who will share with Him the important work of spiritual formation and disciple-making. What should these team teachers be like?

TEACHERS IN THE CHURCH

When it comes to the world, we can lead people where we haven't been. Just consider GPS and the how-to-do-it voices all around us. But it's impossible to lead somebody where we haven't been when it relates to spiritual things. Teachers in the church need to have been a disciple taught by the Spirit of God, have an intimate and ongoing relationship with Jesus, and personally know the vigor of life transformation. They need to understand how their lives have been transformed and be able to explain the processes clearly to others. Along with this, they should share what they've learned regarding the spiritual disciplines that bring people into God's presence so He can work in their lives. They need an ongoing attachment to the Vine.

Our perspective today tends to be that people are qualified to teach if they have a great deal of knowledge about a subject. However, the Hebrew word for "knowledge" (*da'at* derived from the verb *yada*) is much more intimate and personal than our understanding of the word. We say we "know" someone and may use the term rather lightly for a simple acquaintance. For the Jewish people, however, this word was used only if they had a personal and intimate relationship with the individual. Thus a teacher shouldn't simply know about God with head knowledge but have a deep relationship with Him.

Besides knowledge, teachers should also demonstrate wisdom. Again, the Hebrew root word for *wisdom* was ascribed to a person who could separate between right and wrong, good

> *Those who are gifted by God to oversee the incredible forming current will have these gifts of knowledge, wisdom, and understanding.*

and bad, left and right, up and down. God will provide anointed teachers in the church with wisdom to discern. Such individuals won't just "parrot" information handed down to them but will have sifted through it, discovered and weighed it. They'll be able to see through something that is "off" and point out worldly or demonic aspects of thinking, trends, and activities. This gifting is vitally important in our churches today.

Teachers should have understanding. The Hebrew root word for *understanding* is *banah*, which means "to build." If something is to be constructed, then the construction processes must be discerned. A teacher gifted by God can break something down, point out its parts, see the process that should be used to fix it or construct it, and share this with others. In this sense, teachers called by God may point out areas that need to be repaired or built up in order for individuals and the church as a whole to be strong.

Those who are gifted by God to oversee the incredible forming current will have these gifts of knowledge, wisdom, and understanding. The Lord needs people who have walked as committed disciples themselves and are willing to impart what they've learned to others. It's a serious undertaking—one not to be taken lightly.

Disciples will listen to their teachers, but if the teachers are prideful, uncommitted, or just plain wrong, the results can be serious. "Jesus said to his disciples: 'Things that cause people to stumble are bound to come, but woe to anyone through whom they come. It would be better for them to be thrown into the sea with a millstone tied around their neck than to cause one of these little ones to stumble. So watch yourselves'" (Luke 17:1–3).

Teachers must be careful not to share untruth. Even what sounds fine at first glance must be scrutinized. Likewise, if they're holding unredeemed, sinful areas in their lives, this can have an adverse effect on those they teach. The pupils might feel that if their beloved teacher can act in a certain way, even though sinful, they can do the same. Students easily "catch" attitudes from their teachers including sarcasm, haughtiness, faithlessness, rationalization, and cynicism.

James 3:1 makes a rather startling statement: "Not many of you should become teachers, my fellow believers, because you know that we who teach will be judged more strictly." After reading verses like these, one is tempted never to teach, but this isn't God's intention. He doles out teaching gifts to strengthen the church and keep it on the right track. The body needs to appreciate and utilize such gifts. God knows we need these gifted men and women! At the same time, no one should presume to take on the role of teacher without an anointing and calling from God, which includes more than a head full of information.

METHODOLOGIES

Abundant methodologies are available for the teacher who is called by God and has humbly accepted the service. There are many ways to go about the process of teaching and learning. An anointed teacher is able to use a good many of them as needed and as led by the Holy Spirit. Selection depends upon what is useful so the learner can grow. Inflexible and boring styles that turn off learners aren't part of God's repertoire.

Certainly there are times when the teacher needs to provide information. In fact, basic information must be assimilated before a person can move on to higher levels of thinking. This is all right for a time. However, a teacher isn't meant to be a permanent sage-on-a-stage. First of all, this is too distanced from the learner. Secondly, it provides a risk of pride and arrogance on the part of the teacher. (I have the information and I-who-know-it-all will dispense this to you.) The methodologies used by Christian teachers should instead model those of Jesus.

He never taught with an attitude of pride but with humility. He taught in ways that made people think, utilizing examples in the world around Him. He told stories and parables. These were remembered and applied long after the lesson. He asked questions and got people to talk and share what was in their hearts. He didn't distance Himself from the people but interacted with them to show them how to live. Jesus exemplified the life of His Father.

Likewise, Jesus wasn't afraid to meddle. Teaching includes some evaluation, and it entails sharing the truth so the person can change and grow. Consider that He nailed the crux of the problems with the rich young ruler, the woman at the well, Peter's denial, Nicodemus, and others—the list could go on and on. He cared enough to speak the truth and allow the person to make a choice to be transformed or not.

This choice-giving was always a part of Jesus' teaching. Nicodemus had to decide if he would be born again. The rich young ruler had to determine how fervently he wanted to follow Jesus. God isn't a King who coerces and browbeats people into submission. Rather He's a loving Father who nurtures, guides, cultivates and prunes, waters and nourishes, persuades and reasons. He doesn't use force.

As a patient guide, Jesus shows us what to do and say. He initiates action, shares His knowledge generously, doesn't upbraid us when we ask questions, and is kind throughout the process. He

> *Godly teachers apply the Scriptures to things that are pertinent to their students right then and there.*

wants us to spend time listening to Him and learning the construct for the work of His kingdom.

Jesus was also excellent at disassembling cultural and religious products. He could point out that something was wrong and then provide the alternative. Although He was often put on the defensive by the Pharisees and Sadducees with questions meant to trap Him, He was ready with a wise answer, many times accompanied by a question given in return. He had an astute mind and wasn't afraid to take on untruth. Jesus spoke what the Father wanted Him to speak. He functioned well in the midst of the current events of His time.

One of my favorite stories in Scripture is found in Luke 24. Here we have two of Jesus' disciples walking from Jerusalem to Emmaus on the evening of His resurrection. Suddenly, Jesus (in His resurrected body) came alongside them, but they didn't recognize Him. He asked what they were talking about and Cleopas got a little saucy with his answer. "Are you the only one visiting Jerusalem who does not know the things that have happened there in these days?" (v. 18).

When you stop and think about this, it's almost hilarious. Cleopas was basically saying (in our modern-day lingo): "What? Haven't you turned on the TV and watched the news? Is your computer broken? How can you *not* know what's been going on?" But he was saying this to Jesus, who knew far more than Cleopas did!

Jesus didn't wear His knowledge on His sleeve, however. He asked, "What things?" (v. 19).

Of course, the two disciples spouted off what they knew about Jesus . . . *to* Jesus! They went on and on. Finally, Jesus said they were foolish and slow of heart to believe all that the prophets had spoken, and He "explained to them what was said in all the Scriptures concerning himself" (v. 27). That must have been quite a teaching session!

As they reached Emmaus, Jesus acted like He would go further, but they begged Him to stay with them. If they had not done so, they would never have known it was Jesus. We, too, have to seek the Lord and yearn for Him and invite Him to participate in our lives. If we give Him that chance, He'll reveal Himself. And that's exactly what Jesus did during supper time.

When He then disappeared, they said, "Were not our hearts burning within us while he talked with us on the road and opened the Scriptures to us?" (v. 32).

Jesus was excellent at opening the Scriptures to them. He opened both their minds and their hearts in the process. He explained what the prophets had said and made it all obvious, providing understanding and insight.

This is what teachers who are gifted by God do. They are well-informed about Scriptures, but they don't simply teach the bare facts and settle with reciting details accurately. Godly teachers apply the Scriptures to things that are pertinent to their students right then and there. They have the latest news and know the fads and trends, and they can share God's perspective on this from their knowledge and their experience. They sense through the Spirit what people need.

A good teacher can teach for an hour or more and when finished, the listeners are apt to say, "What? Done already? I could listen all night!" That's because the lesson spoken from God is life-giving, life-changing, and life-applicable. It makes our hearts burn.

I love to listen to a gifted teacher. They can explain a passage of Scripture in a way I've never seen before, even though I've read it a thousand times. A good teacher brings a Bible story to life, and people feel like they're right there in the historical setting. The students hear information that suddenly makes everything clear. They walk away changed on the inside, which ultimately brings about changed behavior in the body of Christ. The Word has come alive and been applied. What a gift to the church!

TYPES OF TEACHERS

The teaching gift emerges in many ways in the church. It's possible we haven't viewed everyone with a type of teaching gift as being in this category. We tend to formalize teaching and think that the great and well-educated teacher who can stand in front of a classroom and exude information without notes is the only type of teacher there is. Of course, we need this kind of teacher. Ezra is a good example. We are told that Ezra "had devoted himself to the study and observance of the Law of the LORD, and to teaching its decrees and laws in Israel" (Ezra 7:10), which brought many people back to God.

However, teaching doesn't always have to be accomplished by a well-known scholar or in a formalized way. It can come through many different people in a variety of packages: (1) a counselor, either a licensed, professional counselor or pastoral counseling; (2) a guide or mentor; (3) a life coach; (4) a facilitator of specialized groups such as marriage encounters or Bible study groups; (5) having lunch with someone to help them work out a problem; (6) training workers of special needs groups; (7) teaching a new converts class or membership course; (8) writing or blogging devotionals; (9) teaching workshops at retreats; (10) leading boys' and girls' clubs and youth programs; (11) teaching Sunday school; (12) facilitating a small group; (13) working with Bible quiz; (14) leading a mothers' gathering or a women's meeting or a men's group; (15) preparing and writing curriculum; and (16) teaching a Bible course at a Christian college or seminary. All of these are likely to provide opportunities for teaching and discipleship, though this isn't automatic and must be purposely incorporated.

With so many teaching options available (and there are more), the number of people we need to be gifted by God in teaching is huge. Yet it's often difficult to find people for some of these positions. The challenge isn't a lack of people with teaching and discipleship abilities within the church. The problem is that we have to be careful who we count as teachers—for their sakes, for ours, and for the sakes of those they teach. Many potential teachers aren't ready to teach, though they could be if we helped them.

It's a difficult cycle to break. We need people who've gone through a strong discipleship process to teach potential teachers. If those who should be teaching are missing huge chunks of learning themselves, what do we do? Perhaps part of the answer is that the whole church should be challenged to enter a radical forming process without which it will surely be weak and lax in passing on Christianity to the next generation of believers. Statistics indicate this very problem right now.

KNOWING AND FOLLOWING JESUS

We need far more people who've definitely and completely chosen to follow Jesus. People who've committed their lives entirely to Him and have submitted themselves to be at His disposal for anything He might ask of them. Who are willing to lay down everything to be taught and formed by the Savior and become an ongoing disciple no matter what it costs.

This goes for everyone, leaders as well. It has to. Everyone has to follow. When the leaders are overwhelmed with following close on the heels of Jesus, it will then seep down to the rest of the church. Leonard Sweet, in his book *I Am a Follower*, which we discussed earlier, has an important point to make:

> This is the great tragedy of the church in the last fifty years. We have changed Paul's words, "Follow me as I follow Christ," to "Follow me as I lead for Christ." Over and over we hear, "What the church needs is more and better leaders," or "Training leaders is job one."
>
> Really?
>
> Jesus said, "Go and make disciples." We *stopped* and built worship warehouses.
>
> Jesus said, "Follow me." We heard, "Be a leader."
>
> Paul said, "Do the work of an evangelist." We've done the work of a marketer.
>
> Somewhere back in the past half century, we diagnosed the church's problem as a crisis of leading, not a crisis of following. It's as if we read Bonhoeffer's *Cost of Discipleship* and decided we'd rather talk about something else entirely.[18]

God is the master teacher, and He wants us to learn directly from Him. Whatever brings us into His presence so He can teach us is our responsibility. At the very least, we have to get ourselves into His classroom. Teachers should be walking out of their own class of the Spirit before they start teaching students.

God has much to share with us. As we practice the various spiritual disciplines of Bible reading, prayer, and reflection, we find that we (the branches) become attached to Him (the Vine). We must learn to remain in Him because only as we stay attached to the vine will we bear fruit.

The foundational work of discipleship is to help people stay attached to Jesus and maintain an intimate relationship with Him. Nothing can replace this. Students and teachers alike shouldn't confuse Christian consumerism of books, conferences, and ideas with the presence of God. Nothing can replace being in His presence and being obedient. We can't perpetuate the myth that we can live nice Christian lives and not bring Christ into it.

Salvation is more than saying a prayer; it's becoming an obedient follower. A. W. Tozer expressed his "feeling that a notable heresy has come into being throughout evangelical Christian circles—the widely accepted concept that we humans can choose to accept Christ only because we need him as Savior and that we have the right to postpone our obedience to Him as Lord as long as we want to." He goes on to state that "salvation apart from obedience is unknown in the sacred scriptures."[19]

THE SPIRITUAL JOB OF TEACHERS

Smith Wigglesworth had a prayer that went like this: "Word of God, press in on my heart that the Spirit might press it out of me in Jesus' name. May I not simply quote Scripture to those I meet every day, but may I rather impart the life of Christ to those who need Him. Amen."[20]

Teachers must work hard at becoming knowledge set on fire by God. They should be so alive in the Spirit that they draw others toward Jesus in their everyday lives. They should know the Master teacher so well and live so carefully under His guidance that they can readily speak, model, guide, provide insight, have understanding, use wisdom, and show the knowledge of Jesus Christ that comes from an intimate relationship with Him. Through the power of the Holy Spirit and the Word of God, teachers can impart the life of Christ to their pupils.

This is true for every level and type of teaching. University and seminary professors and theologians need this along with Sunday school teachers and counselors and people who mentor and coach. Everybody used by God in the radical forming process must be rooted in God.

Teachers who are anointed by God to lead out this important current should keep to the ancient roots of literacy and study, memorization and learning, writing and speaking. They must be competent to do the painstaking work of integrating faith and knowledge. Teachers should be able to wrestle with cultural changes as needed because they personally know the depths of God. They ought to be adept at leading people into experiencing truth, not just be able to explain it.

The church needs to discover more ways of supporting and appreciating teachers and professors as they seek to be more and more under the anointing of the Holy Spirit. Instead of looking at theologians and professors with suspicion or discomfort, sometimes viewing them as detached and irrelevant, the church should discover old and new ways of incorporating them into the life of the church so the body becomes mature in every respect. We need godly, dedicated teachers!

SCHOLARS AND SAINTS

It would seem to me almost impossible for everyone in the church to be properly discipled if I didn't know two things. The first thing I'm sure of is that no matter how much teaching may be lacking in the church, the Master teacher is always available. If we have a lack of teachers right now, the first step is to encourage people to put themselves in the place where the Master can teach them. Bibles and resources abound, and people can be encouraged to grab hold of the spiritual disciplines and to let Christ instruct them and change them in their inner being.

Second, historically we have seen viable periods of church history where most everything we've been discussing was in evidence. This gives me hope, and although our present day will not and should not exactly replicate historical models of formation, if we listen to God, He'll lead us into new approaches tailor-made for today.

One of my favorite historical periods for a mighty flow of the follow-the-leader current can be found in the Celtic church from St. Patrick on for the next few hundred years. I like it because it entails so many aspects of what is needed to have a strong stream of discipleship in the church. Ireland during this period has been called "the land of saints and scholars." This phrase means that they were both holy people totally committed to God and scholars at the same time.

The monasteries in Ireland generally began with a hermit who went away to pray, fast, study, and be with God. Students soon gathered around these scholar-saints because of who they had become as well as what they knew. These men and women had highly-developed spiritual disciplines of prayer, fasting, study, Scripture reading, simplicity, and worship.

As the Irish monasteries grew (in fact gaining a reputation for being the best schools in all of Europe), they developed a superior education that included all kinds of subjects and content, literature, and languages. The integration of faith and learning was strong, with a robust Christian education that allowed them to deal with worldly perspectives. Out of this came an expansive mission movement that spread out over Europe, where monks were recorded to do miracles and move in the gifts of the Spirit as people came to God.

One of the crucial aspects of this Irish education was that each student was provided with an *anam chara*, which translated from Gaelic means "soul friend." This person came alongside the student, was their spiritual advisor, and "meddled" with their sin, and the two got to know each other well. The *anam chara* guided the student's development and provided wisdom regarding critical points in their ministry. Students often traveled many miles later in life to keep in touch with their *anam chara*, especially as life-changes were in the air.

I believe that God is so desirous of this radical forming current to be unstopped and flow strongly again that He is ready to provide a new and fresh perspective regarding it. Listen . . . and learn. He may want to use you as a teacher to help lead this current in your church. And when He chooses you as a teacher, remember to be like Paul and go through any pains, even into travail, to see Christ formed in those individuals He puts into your keeping.

THINGS TO CONSIDER . . .

1. Teaching people to obey everything Jesus commanded (Matt. 28:20) is part of the Great Commission, and so it is just as essential to the life and vitality of the church as evangelism. Given this, do you think your church is paying enough attention to teaching? What could be done to strengthen this aspect of the Great Commission?

2. In the world people think that a great deal of knowledge about a subject is all that's necessary to teach it. Chapter six explores the concept that Christian teachers need more. They should have developed their character, their spirituality, their own formation, and their link with God. They must have been personally taught by God before trying to teach others about Him. Do you agree with this? Why or why not?

3. This chapter describes a number of different ways that the teaching gift is used in the church. What programs and people do you see involved in this gifting in your own church?

4. Do you think you have a strong enough pool of people in your church who are fully-formed Christians following Jesus all the way? This is the pool from which we should be drawing the teachers. If this pool is not big enough, what can be done about it?

5. Do you think, as Leonard Sweet suggests, that we have changed Paul's words, "Follow me as I follow Christ," to "Follow me as I lead for Christ"? If so, what changes do we need to make?

6. How effective are the spiritual disciplines in your own life? How might they be improved?

7. Do you see a lot of spiritual fruit in your life because you have learned to "remain in the vine"? If you wish there were more, what can you do about it?

8. Do you have a personal *anam chara*? If not, who might be able to fulfill this role of "soul friend" and teacher in your life?

Chapter Seven

THE SYNCHRONIZED CHOREOGRAPHY CURRENT

Romans 12:10 admonishes us: "In love of the brethren be tenderly affected one to another; in honor preferring one another" (ASV). In order to be the kind of church God wants us to be, we must learn what it actually means to prefer one another. To prefer others takes work and consideration, but the church as a whole is much better when we do it.

When I think of preferring others, the image that always comes to mind is of the Three Musketeers in the classic novel by Alexandre Dumas.[21] I can see them standing with their arms on each other's shoulders. They are wearing their tall leather boots and medieval jackets and hats with the big floppy brim and plume. Aramis takes off his hat, bows low, and says, "After you."

"No! No!" Porthos counters, taking off his hat and sweeping it out as he bows low. "After you!" So Athos steps out; it is his turn.

This is a vivid picture of how the church is meant to function. Love isn't a wishy-washy, idealized dream but rather is practically expressed in a wide variety of ways, both big and small, on an on-going basis. We can't do this well unless we take to heart the Romans 12 verse that tells us to prefer one another. It means stepping back, allowing the other person to take center stage, thinking of another before ourselves, and moving away

> God wants us to have an interactive relationship with Him and then with each other in the church.

from our stubbornness, selfishness, and the mistaken belief that we're always right.

The best model of this is the Trinity. The Greek noun *perichoresis* was the favorite word of the early church to describe the interrelationship of the Trinity. It denotes the deep fellowship that Father, Son, and Holy Spirit have in their relationship with each other. The more we study this, the more we will be amazed by our Trinitarian God, who models how we should all get along in the church.

An in-depth study of Scripture regarding this concept would take a great deal of space but just to mention a few examples: (1) Jesus said it was good that He was going away because otherwise the Holy Spirit wouldn't come (John 16:7); (2) When Jesus was baptized, the Holy Spirit came in the form of a dove and the Father expressed His pleasure (Luke 3:21–22); (3) Jesus said that He only spoke what His Father wanted Him to say, that He only did what He saw His Father doing, and that He did nothing on His own initiative (multiple places throughout the gospel of John); (4) the Spirit searches and then shares the mind of God (1 Cor. 2:10b–11).

Scripture clearly shows us that God the Father, the Holy Spirit, and the Son all work together well, preferring one another. They need each other and rely on one another. They give, and they receive from the other members of the Godhead. What a beautiful thing! The Trinity is a unified team.

The *perichoresis* concept is that each person of the Godhead indwells the other. This indwelling is deep and penetrating.

Each person in the Trinity makes space for the others (like the Celtic trinity knot), prefers the others, and glorifies the others. In John 17:1, just before He went to the cross, Jesus said, "Father, the hour has come. Glorify your Son, that your Son may glorify you." And in John 16:14, Jesus said that the Holy Spirit "will glorify me because it is from me that he will receive what he will make known to you." The love experienced through the fellowship of the Godhead brings glory one to the other. We have more of the Father and of Jesus when we have more of the Spirit. This is true with each member of the Trinity; each gives us more of the others.

Interestingly, there is no absorption of one member by another but individuality is retained. Each accomplishes certain acts as it is their turn at different times. This deep sharing doesn't require an erasure of variety and differences in function. Each retains their distinctive identity, and God wants that for us also.

Many people hesitate to become Christians because they think they'll lose their individuality within the expectations of the church. Instead, the church should strive to be the place where individuality is appreciated and nurtured, because we need all different types of people to accomplish what God wants.

Will Davis, Jr. said in his book *10 Things Jesus Never Said: And Why You Should Stop Believing Them*: "Give other Christians permission to be different from you. You're not the only Christ-follower in the world, and neither are you the most committed. Your way of loving Jesus is neither the only way nor the best. If you don't know that, your Christian world is way too small."[22]

God wants us to have an interactive relationship with Him and then with each other in the church. We are to be a living and loving organism, not a fighting machine that wreaks havoc on itself. We are neither a center of disagreement, competition, and self-exaltation, nor a place of conformity where individual gifts and personalities are stifled and constrained rather than celebrated and engaged.

In John 17:17–23 Jesus prayed a most gripping prayer in light of what we've been considering. He began by praying for His disciples but then He prayed for more believers after that:

> Sanctify them by the truth; your word is truth. As you sent me into the world, I have sent them into the world. For them I sanctify myself, that they too may be truly sanctified. My prayer is not for them alone. I pray also for those who will believe in me through their message, that all of them may be one, Father, just are you are in me and I am in you. May they also be in us so that the world may believe that you have sent me. I have given them the glory that you gave me, that they may be one as we are one—I in them and you in me—so that they may be brought to complete unity. Then the world will know that you sent me and have loved them even as you have loved me.

The first sentence reminds us that Jesus does His sanctifying work within us as He brings the same kind of oneness and unity that the Trinity experiences. He even shares His glory with us! And when His glory is on the church, bringing us into complete unity, it lets the world know that God the Father sent His Son and that He loves the church just as He loves Jesus. This is God's way of drawing people to Himself.

The word *perichoresis*, although not in Scripture, was used often in the writings of the early church fathers. The first part is from the Greek word *peri*, which means "around." The second part comes from the word out of which we derive "choreography." It's the word *khoreia*, which means "making room for, rotating around, or dance."

We get that bowing idea of the Three Musketeers again. The relationship between the three members of the Trinity was described by early Christians as an eternal, holy dance of each member around the other two. It allows space for the others to move, while being aware of each other's movements and being ready to respond. I believe this image will be instructive for us as we consider the church and its care.

THE GREAT DANCE

Perelandra, the second book in C. S. Lewis's science fiction trilogy, has a memorable scene that Lewis calls "The Great Dance." In the early part of the story, the main character, Ransom, has accomplished what he was supposed to do for the planet Venus. He has fought the evil personified in Professor Weston (who insidiously had been trying to tempt the young Eve character of *Perelandra*), and Ransom has won.

In the last chapter there's a celebratory time in which Ransom is dialoguing with the king and queen of Venus and leaders from other planets. They're stating some astute perspectives on God and the universe in a sort of doxology—the whole of which is insightful regarding the nature of God. That doxology still rings in my soul! Suddenly his eyes see it all as a Great Dance:

> And now, by a transition which he did not notice, it seemed that what had begun as speech was turned into sight, or into something that can be remembered only as if it were seeing. He thought he saw the Great Dance. It seemed to be woven out of the intertwining undulation of many cords or bands of light, leaping over and under one another and mutually embraced in arabesques and flower-like subtleties. Each figure as he looked at it became the master-figure or focus of the whole spectacle, by means of which his eye disentangled all

else and brought it into unity—only to be itself entangled when he looked to what he had taken for mere marginal decorations and found that there also the same hegemony was claimed, and the claim made good, yet the former pattern not thereby dispossessed but finding in its new subordination a significance greater than that which it had abdicated.[23]

We sometimes yearn to be in the center of the choreography because it seems so wonderful. In other instances, we're shy to go there—wishing that someone else would do what we find so difficult and costly to accomplish. In those times when God asks us to be in the middle of things, we ought to accept (whether for an exciting assignment or a difficult one). We should seek to fulfill whatever God has called us to do. He will go with us, and we should not be shy.

Likewise, just because we have the main spot for a while, doesn't mean we need to keep it. Many times people manipulate and fight for center stage. However, in the dance of life, we're all meant to have our time in the middle of the action and then, when our stint is done, to get out gracefully and let someone else have that spot. Our subordination (as Lewis states so beautifully) is still important and part of the whole picture. God, the primary choreographer, gives us a fresh place in the dance and doesn't leave us out.

In the Great Dance, each factor has its value. Even though we don't understand it all, everything done in ministry is thoroughly intertwined and each individual entity contributes to the whole. Likewise, each cannot do their part without the rest. Lewis says:

In the plan of the Great Dance plans without number interlock, and each movement becomes in its season the breaking into flower of the whole design to which all else had been directed. Thus each is equally at the center and none are there by being equals, but some by giving place and some by receiving it, the small things by their smallness and the great by their greatness, and all the patterns linked and looped together by the unions of a kneeling with a sceptred love. Blessed be He![24]

In the world today, many people are hurt when they have to give up center stage. Famous actors, athletes, CEOs, all sorts of leaders in various kinds of places, including ministers at times, find it almost excruciating to think they have to step off the stage for one reason or another. However, no person was ever meant to monopolize the arena.

God help us to know when to give it up gracefully! Only a decisive ego with a proud heart would try to hold center stage forever. Ask John the Baptist about that temptation. Ask Moses who was left on the mountain just within sight of the Promised Land. Ask Jesus who abandoned the center of everything in heaven to come down to earth for a while.

The point of our service in the church isn't how much we do and how important we are. The point is whether or not we're taking our place in the synchronized dance that God is orchestrating. When each one takes their assigned role, the design is fabulous! When one wants to do their own thing, needing attention, wanting to hog the show, or playing to the crowd, disaster ensues.

LETTING GO AND EXPERIENCING CHANGE

If we would all embrace the concept of letting go and taking a step back, we would be much better off. There are things that just need to slough off our bodies such as dead skin, toxins, and waste, and this goes for life in general. Many times we grieve and throw a fit when God takes something away from us. He's just doing it for our own good; pruning us a little bit.

> *We must first put down what we know before we can pick up what we haven't yet tried.*

This goes for individual believers and for the church as a whole. The church is meant to be organic, alive, growing, and changing. Sometimes it's difficult to make the changes we should because someone has clutched on to a program and is holding it too tightly. At times the person doesn't need to change, but what they oversee does. Unfortunately, people often take it as an affront when others ask them to modify or transform something they lead.

I remember in one church where I ministered I said: "What would happen if you just had a big funeral service for everything you're currently doing in the church? Bury it all! Then start afresh. Think about what your people require. How can this best be accomplished? We don't have to do it the same way over and over and over again!" Programs ought to be based upon what people need to grow in their Christian lives and not be established upon tradition, habit, or rote. People change and so should the church, as the Spirit directs.

Once I was asked to lead an all-day women's prayer meeting at a church, but they experienced a crisis and called me to cancel. I knew it was the time to pray and asked what was stopping them. They said they didn't have the energy to do the nice brunch they generally laid out for the event. I suggested they just plunk down some donuts in a box with some orange juice and paper cups and let it go at that. We had the best prayer meeting that day! We can let go of "stuff" all over the place and let God do something fresh and new. Too often, we're prone to make things far too complicated.

To be honest, many of us find change unnerving. Rather than embracing these times, we often find it difficult to make the necessary modifications to navigate the shifting waters successfully.

Numerous dysfunctional outcomes can result from change: denial, anger (demonstrated overtly or subtly concealed), a sense of loss, mourning, refusing to move ahead into the next phase, holding onto the past as an ideal, withdrawal, shifting blame to others, missing God's best timing, demonstrating fear or annoyance.

Part of the problem seems to be our inability to lay down past things so we can pick up new ones. The old is comfortable and we understand it. Therefore, setting it aside before we can experience what it's like to pick up the new is unsettling. It strikes at our sense of importance and security. We want to try things out while holding onto the past. However, we rarely have this opportunity. We must first put down what we know before we can pick up what we haven't yet tried. If we attempt to hold both, we'll fumble them both.

The church today has a challenge. We can't lose our ancient roots of truth. On the other hand, we can surely let go of a wide variety of optional practices, attitudes, and customs. These are keeping us from renewal, from being the active body of Christ that God intends. Simultaneously holding a rootedness in God and finding a creative expression of His love and work today is what makes for a healthy church.

TOO BUSY TO HEAR

God will lead us as we search out His plan and will. He's the One who holds our hands, not the other way around. When He holds on, we can't slip out. But to do this, we have to be beside Him, within reach of His hand and the sound of His voice.

Some are too busy trying to fix things, bogged down by activities, and meddling in affairs that God never called them to do. If people are too occupied to spend time with God, they've taken on some responsibilities He didn't give them. A recent Barna survey shows that Bible readers who say their number one frustration is never having enough time to read the Bible rose from 40 to 47 percent within the last year.[25]

When we don't have time to spend with God, the work gets old, and we rush through it rather than finding fresh insight from Him. We get tired because He isn't in the work we've set ourselves to do. And, perhaps worst of all, it's likely we've missed out on the work He most ardently wants us to do.

We need to let some things go. Set them down. Be refreshed in His presence, and then see what He wants in the here and now. He cares so much about us, not just what we're doing.

In his book *Soul Keeping*, John Ortberg says, "We all commit idolatry every day. It is the sin of the soul meeting its needs with anything that distances it from God."[26] The Lord wants us to come to Him so we can be healthy and whole. Then we'll be good, strong participants in the choreography He's designed for us.

If no one takes directions from the choreographer, everything is a mess. Everything! We must each pay attention to what God is saying. Colossians 1:18 states that Jesus "is the head of the body, the church." He wants us to let Him be in charge. We need to bow to His role in the body. Each individual in the church needs to listen to and obey the head. A lot of church problems would disappear if this were the case.

The manner by which we come into agreement is often to stop our bickering and pray. The head of the church isn't going to tell opposing things to different people. He wants to bring unity and choreographed organization to the body. If we mind Him, everything falls into place.

A LIVING ORGANISM VERSUS A MACHINE

In the organism called the church, the lifeblood comes from Jesus. The living essence in believers and the church comes from within, not from without. It isn't imposed but wells up from the inner being. The Spirit breathes in us and guides our thinking and our doing. Ray Steadman, in his well-known classic, *Body Life*, stated:

> The church is not to be a conglomeration of individuals who happen to agree on certain ideas. It is bound together as an organism in a bodily unity. It is true that a body is an organization but it is much more than an organization. The essence of a body is that it consists of thousands of cells with one mutually shared life. . . . It is the sharing of life that makes a body different from an organization. An organization derives power from the association of individuals, but a body derives power from the sharing of life.[27]

As we in the body of Christ work together and all of us conscientiously keep the flow open to God, we'll more rapidly agree on what is the mind of Christ. He wants to share with us what we're supposed to do together, how and when. With God as the chief choreographer, our task is to be enlivened by Him to accomplish our part in the big picture through the power of His Spirit.

We should listen individually, and then we should listen corporately as the church. Otherwise, the choreography doesn't get synchronized. It is critical that we come together first as the people of God before we do the work of God![28]

Chuck Miller discusses the importance of opening all business and other meetings and training sessions in prayer, spending time together in God's Word, sharing time together first.[29] We are a community first of all, and if we forget this, our differences loom larger than they should and we all become tense. As we take time to be together with Him, we can more rapidly discern the mind of Christ collectively.

We have some tendencies in the church that aren't in keeping with what we've been advocating here. One is that we may decide what we want to do and then ask God to bless it (Saul). Another is that we may really hear from God about what He wants but then we head out on our own and try to establish it in our own strength or share it too soon (Joseph). Yet another is that we don't wait for His perfect timing (Sarah and Abraham).

All of these approaches attempt to set the things of God in motion without Him. This is tiring, wearing, and probable trouble. The synchronized choreography current only flows out of God Himself. Without that, there is dryness. We aren't the choreographers; God is.

When we move out in our own strength, without being invigorated and empowered by the Holy Spirit, we often expend energy on things that don't matter and won't produce much for God's kingdom . It isn't that we don't mean well. However, we may miss the humbler but greater work of the kingdom. "You are the Body of Christ," said St. Augustine in an Easter sermon in the fourth century. "In you and through you the work of the incarnation must go forward. You are to be taken. You are to be blessed, broken and distributed, that you may be the means of grace and vehicles of eternal love."

That is what the church is all about, and God helps us, but perhaps we've missed some of it because we've been too busy doing what He didn't ask for us to do. We are meant to care for and give out to others in the church, in our neighborhoods, and at work. Jesus walked about doing good everywhere He went, and so should we.

THE GIFTS OF THE SPIRIT

One way God intends to keep the body healthy and to touch people who don't know Him is through the supernatural gifts of the Spirit. An idea that is often inferred or stated is that members of the body of Christ are given a gift of the Spirit in which they are expected to operate.

Now it is true that we all inherently work more in certain spiritual gifts than in others because of how we're wired. However, I believe that any of us in the body of Christ could and may be called upon by the Spirit to be used in any of the gifts if God chooses. The gifts aren't inherent in just a couple of people; they are distributed.

Further, God wants us to give away the gifts of the Spirit. The gifts aren't for us but are to be passed on to the recipient. For example, if God uses us in the gift of healing, the person we pray for is healed, not us. Or if He uses us in the gift of wisdom, the other person receives the wisdom. When He uses us in the gift of tongues, it is to benefit the body. This means that as God distributes a spiritual gift, we had better pass it on to the recipient(s). It isn't ours to keep or to stop. We must give it away or the people it was meant to profit won't receive the benefit.

The wonderful purpose of the gifts of the Spirit is to keep the body strong and healthy. Together they provide encouragement, confirmation, healing, relief, direction, faith, and so much more. "Now to each one the manifestation of the Spirit is given for the common good" (1 Cor. 12:7).

Recently someone made an observation saying, "The churches are still functioning, but there's no Physician present, it seems." How people are yearning for a fresh visitation of the Spirit's renewal and power! In order to have a healthy body, the Spirit wants free sway to speak and act, and the gifts are one of the main ways He accomplishes this. Human efforts to help people will result in only a shadow of what the Holy Spirit can do.

Jesus moved constantly in the gifts of the Spirit during His time on earth, providing space for the Spirit to work and modeling how we should bow to the Spirit's operations.

As 1 Corinthians 12:4–6 explains, there are many different gifts of the Spirit, varieties of workings, service and activities, but God is the One who activates all of them among the believers. Obviously if we're supposed to benefit from the gifts of the Spirit, we have to be connected to the body in church. Being separate doesn't allow the other members to give to us or for us to give to them.

Hebrews 10:25 warns us not to give up "meeting together, as some are in the habit of doing," but instead to go on "encouraging one another—and all the more as you see the Day approaching." I think the Day is approaching, and certainly this isn't the time to forsake gathering together. The body must have all the parts in order to function the way it was meant to. In order for this current to flow freely, the body has to come together and not have individual stragglers.

Dwight L. Moody once said, "Church attendance is as vital to a disciple as a transfusion of rich, healthy blood to a sick man."[30] If we want a strong body, we have to be willing to minister to each other—practically, lovingly, and supernaturally. We should long to receive these things and to place ourselves regularly in the church work and services so we can all do this. It's a powerful give-and-take that the Lord designed.

God wants us all together so He can synchronize our efforts. To synchronize something is to cause things to agree in time or to make things happen with the same timing and speed. As we take ourselves into the Lord's presence, both separately and then together, He will accomplish this. Perhaps it seems almost impossible, but with God, nothing is impossible.

He will slow down some people and speed up others until they come into unity. As we pray, He changes people's minds, softens hearts, and helps them to agree. He hands out assignments and assists each person to be comfortable with their role. He allows us to help, encourage, and support each other in our duties and to prefer one another.

When the living, organic church works together to affect our world, watch out! And this is exactly what God wants to do right now . . . smack dab in the midst of our postmodern challenges. Let's stop looking mainly at organization and start focusing more on the life of the organism. God is ready to do amazing things with His church. We just need to listen to Him.

THINGS TO CONSIDER . . .

1. In this chapter the author discussed the Greek word *perichoresis* and how God the Father, the Holy Spirit, and the Son all work together well, preferring one another. How do you see each member of the Trinity cooperating, supporting one another, deeply in fellowship, giving space to each other to do their own unique work?

2. The passage in C. S. Lewis's *Perelandra* that talks about "The Great Dance" indicates that we must be ready to step into and out of the middle of the circle. How do we get more comfortable with a team approach?

3. Why is it so difficult for us to relinquish certain things and embrace change? Is your church flexible and growing? What about you as an individual?

4. Do you think we're spending enough time listening to the Lord and discovering what He wants for the church now? Or are we too busy perpetuating our programs to hear what He has in mind that is fresh and new?

5. Do you think the church in general allows for the differences of its members? What can we do to better appreciate and celebrate individuals and their distinct contributions?

6. Is the church more apt to be thought of as an organization, a sort of machine, or as an organic, living organism? Explain.

7. How effectively are the gifts of the Spirit being experienced in your own church? In what ways do you see the ministry of the gifts of the Spirit contributing to the health of the church as a whole?

Chapter Eight

THE PASTOR

T he calling of the pastor is to oversee the church so it stays an organic, on-the-move, healthy, lively, synchronized body. This isn't an easy task.

Pastors are responsible to see that the body of Christ is full of His lifeblood; and if not, then a transfusion is in order. If the church isn't full of Jesus and attached to each member of the Trinity, then the pastor needs to do something about that. A pastor's main concern should be whether or not the body—corporately and individually—is attached to Jesus so His life can provide sustenance, energy, and empowerment. Sometimes, however, the pastor is the one who needs that recharge of lifeblood and an infusion of hope.

Many pastors are worn out, weary with the rat race, and even tired of people. But pastoral ministry is a marathon and not a sprint. Pacing is important; pastors should look at the long haul and not burn themselves out today. Thankfully, the pastor isn't responsible for all of the currents of the church. God has appointed others to help do the work, and the Lord Himself is there. Still, the task of pastoring can be extremely demanding.

Unfortunately, members of the body sometimes try to destroy each other. Often this happens when the body has become too

> *Pastors need to find fresh love and new ways to care and share, and only the Lord can give that.*

ingrown and self-focused, even to the point of loathing itself. This can be like cutting or other self-injury. If you hear people complaining about their church all the time, perhaps the body is at this stage. The self-harm can be related to intense feelings of anger or frustration, not fitting in, or poor self-image.

If the church is moving out as it should, it doesn't have time for backbiting. The church needs to be encouraged to be part of the solution to problems, to be authentic, to communicate their frustrations to the pastor or others who can help, to practice forgiveness, to bear with differences of opinion and perspective, and to see themselves as Christ sees them.

When the body is healthy, it will be active. It will reach out to others, serve the community, work, laugh, and play together. There will be change, repair, and growth. When it isn't healthy, the body tends to sit and wither away, to atrophy.

Atrophy is the "wasting away" of a part of the body. Causes can include poor circulation, inadequate nourishment, problems with nerve supply, disease, broken bones, as well as disuse or lack of fitness. Pastors are meant to encourage exercise (work for the kingdom), watch for disease or wrong doctrine (mutation), help people know each other (circulation), repair rifts in the body of Christ (bone breaks), re-open communication (nerve problems), and provide and foster nourishment. They will stave off attack by any kind of negative person (wolves) or situations that are dangerous.

As pastors spend time with God, He will indicate what the people require and ways to provide it to them. He will also show pastors how to spend their time, who should get attention, which places are weak, and what to emphasize. All of this is constantly shifting since the body is alive and different parts may have unique needs at various times.

The Holy Spirit will help pastors and the church live for God and produce the fruit of the Spirit. This will develop a body that is truly loving, kind, long-suffering, joyful, peaceful, faithful, gentle, and self-controlled. What a lovely church to serve. People will be drawn to such a group in our fractured world—which is the whole idea.

PASTORAL CARE

Pastors are the ones who will evidence so much of the fruit of the Spirit because they've spent time with Jesus. They love and serve. When there is such a demonstration in the church, others are apt to follow. As in the good shepherd metaphor, the pastor tends the sheep.

Having a caring pastor is a wonderful blessing and relief. When one is ill, a call or a hospital visit from the pastor can mean so much. When a person is grieving, the pastor can be there. When someone is heartsick, what is needed is some extra TLC. At such times, church people and their family members are receptive to the work of God in their lives and will often form their opinions of both God and the church during times of crises.

Pastors need to find fresh love and new ways to care and share, and only the Lord can give that. Their responsibility is to know people in the church by name, to keep contact with them so other church members know what is happening, to note when they're missing, and to be with them when they have needs and tragedies or joys and celebrations. Pastors should understand where people fit in the body, note how they're maturing in the Lord, see the shifts in their lives and their personal growth, and determine if they're still in the best spot(s) for service for them and for the body.

Communication is essential. People must perceive that they are seen, heard, and valued. Preaching from a pulpit is good, of course, but it's one-way communication. What do the parishioners have to say? No, not just about the sermon . . . but about their lives and their fears and their problems. Pastors should stay in touch with what is going on with people, to show them that they care and aren't just trying to patch them up so they can get back to their other work.

The need for true connectivity is increasing all the time. Though social media touts it, true connectivity isn't happening in society today. I noticed this today on my Facebook feed from another twenty-something: "To my über religious friends that I'm still FB friends with. I like you. I want to know what's going on in your life. Seriously—FB is not a platform for witnessing to your less religious friends with scripture verses and testimonials. What's really going on in your life? I actually care . . ."

So many people desire authentic connectivity. We get annoyed when we can't get online; however, I keep talking to people who are also irritated because they feel they aren't able to connect to the pastor or others at the church they attend.

Pastors lead out by caring. They look people in the eye. They make a phone call, or they visit in someone's home. They're reachable and real. Pastors demonstrate to the church how the body is supposed to take care of itself.

Folks today want more than sitting next to one another in a church service and walking away afterwards. They're looking for openness and honesty; people want more of what is genuine and less of what is image. They're searching for a place where they can both give and receive.

Love isn't an option; it's a command. Jesus said, "A new command I give you: Love one another. As I have loved you, so you must love one another. By this everyone will know that you are my disciples, if you love one another" (John 13:34–35). People in our postmodern world yearn to see love in action. The model is totally different from our scraping, self-absorbed world of keeping up with the Joneses.

Pastors have to love enough to do the work of a shepherd: (1) They must use their crook to pull their sheep back from the brink of destruction; (2) they should also use their crooks to draw the sheep close to themselves and the community of believers. They need to let the flock know the shepherd cares for them and wants to spend time with them, and they need to see the sheep assimilated into the flock. (3) The shepherds must be careful to lead the sheep to the Chief Shepherd, Jesus. (4) They should pound the liver out of any destructive element with their rod and not leave their sheep to Satan. (5) Certainly they ought to know when one of their sheep has gone astray and do something about it.

Some pastors have almost become comfortable with a revolving back door. How can this be? What happened to that person we baptized a few months back or that couple we just married? Where are they now?

It probably isn't wise to advocate for any particular size or model of church, but one thing is certain: If pastors can't pastor in the way we've been discussing, then it isn't a suitable model. The body has to remain cared for and healthy. I don't care how big the church is, how many satellites there are, or anything else. Bottom line: Is it a healthy body with personal care for all persons? Does it truly have a pastor and not just a CEO with a grand organizational scheme?

MOVING IN THE SPIRIT

A church that moves in the Spirit does so when the pastor allows. Smith Wigglesworth said, "How the Master can move among the needs and perishing when He has the right of way in the church!"[31]

The Spirit is looking for the freedom to move. Some pastors have perhaps mistaken control for order. Certainly we can do things "in a fitting and orderly way" (1 Cor. 14:40) without controlling the Spirit and retarding His work. We believe that the Holy Spirit is important, but sometimes there's a gap between belief and practice.

The Spirit has to become real in our ministry. He was to Jesus. John the Baptist said he knew it was Jesus he had baptized because he "saw the Spirit come down from heaven as a dove and remain on [Jesus]" (John 1:32). The doves in that region of the Jordan River were wild rock doves. To have one land on your shoulder was a nearly impossible event.

The vibrant Celtic church that started with Saint Patrick had an interesting way of describing Jesus' baptism to the Irish people. Since there were no doves on the island, Patrick decided to explain the Holy Spirit as a wild goose. This is probably a quite accurate analogy since the doves at the Jordan were certainly wild. However, it's a somewhat amusing picture: the wild goose landing on a human shoulder! Of course, with the Holy Spirit, we can always expect the unexpected.

The Holy Spirit doesn't want to be placed in a dovecote and let out when we feel like it. This is control. We're apt to say, "Okay, You can come out now." When we're finished with Him, we put the Holy Spirit back in His cage.

This will not do! Remember, the body needs the mind of Christ, which He shares with us through the Holy Spirit. He is the One who guides into all truth; He also convicts and leads

> *There's no doubt that a Spirit-led church will make the job of the pastor easier.*

to repentance. He teaches all things. Pastors might limit the work of the Spirit, but a healthy body will not be the result.

Instead of restraining the work of the Spirit because they feel awkward, don't know what to do, are afraid or hesitant, pastors should do just the opposite: open up the people to the wonderful, healing, enriching work of the Spirit any time they possibly can. There's no doubt that a Spirit-led church will make the job of the pastor easier.

Therefore, pastors should give time in the services and meetings of the church for the Holy Spirit to move, flow, and fill people, and especially for people to be baptized in the Holy Spirit. God intended for His people to live in this fullness of life. They're going to need it in these last days!

Saint Patrick himself was baptized in the Holy Spirit and spoke in tongues. In his *Confession* he writes about this, and since I'm a Celtic scholar and very interested in this time period, I used my Latin training to check out the original manuscript. Indeed, in the Latin it says that Patrick "spoke with another tongue" and that it was the Spirit of God praying in him.[32] This explains a great deal about the rapid growth of the church of Ireland, which expanded as its leaders worked in miracles, signs and wonders, and the gifts of the Spirit.

The wild goose concept is still a part of Ireland's portrayal of the Holy Spirit, and certainly the Holy Spirit will lead us on some adventures. He cannot be tamed or contained because His work is too important in our world today.

A pastor in New Zealand (who has the wild goose image from Celtic Iona above his altar) shares some reasons this is a fitting symbol for the church:

> The first is that flying in the V formation gives geese a 71 per cent increase in flying range, with flapping wings creating an updraft for the bird following. Flying is a cooperative business.
>
> The second is that the lead goose in the V formation does not, of course, experience this updraft and so tires faster than the others. When the lead goose tires, it rotates back into the formation and another goose takes over the lead.
>
> The third lesson is that when a goose falls out of the formation, it feels the drag and resistance of flying alone and quickly gets back into the formation.
>
> Fourth, when a wild goose is sick or wounded, or shot down, two others follow it to help and protect it until it recovers or dies, while the others continue to fly on. When the goose recovers or dies, a new formation is created, heading in the same direction as the first.
>
> And fifth, when geese are flying in formation, those flying behind honk to encourage those in front to keep up speed.[33]

These points can easily be applied to believers. We can go farther when we do it together. We're meant to share the leadership role, care for the wounded, encourage each other, and take care of those who are weak and hurting. That's what the body of Christ is all about.

PASTORING THE GIFTS OF THE SPIRIT

The gifts of the Spirit are meant to be given to the church, but sometimes the actual working of them can be challenging for pastors. When used properly, the gifts are incredible. Perhaps various pastors feel a little awkward in the operation of some of the gifts, not knowing exactly what to do when these are shared corporately. Then there are the awkward times when human flesh gets mixed up in the delivery and pastors have to try and straighten it out.

Much of the difficulty with moving in the gifts is that people who are spiritually immature attempt to exercise the gifts. They can't discern what is or is not of the Lord because they haven't spent enough time with Him to know His voice. Working out of the flesh certainly creates problems, but the gifts of the Spirit are too valuable to stop up. It would be like burying beautiful diamonds.

So the pastor has the opportunity to correct, facilitate, orchestrate, encourage, and synchronize as the circumstances require. The Spirit doesn't want to be put in a cage. When the human flesh is operating, the Spirit will give the pastor help, wisdom, and authority to know how to handle the situations. I've also seen the Spirit direct people to back down as they were brought to a realization of their wrong desires and pride.

Paul said to the Corinthians, "Since you are eager for gifts of the Spirit, try to excel in those that build up the church" (1 Cor. 14:12). People should be taught that the gifts are to build up the body and to help make it healthy. Instead of asking for every utterance to be cleared, what if we were to say, "If what you feel you have to say to the body doesn't fit these parameters or you have questions or doubts, then let's talk first." This would allow for more of a free and natural flow of the Spirit, and I think it's possible, especially if the body is maturing.

Paul ends this section as follows: "What then shall we say, brothers and sisters? When you come together, each of you has a hymn, or a word of instruction, a revelation, a tongue or an interpretation. Everything must be done so that the church may be built up" (1 Cor. 14:26). Each person joined in. It appears that the early church gatherings had more individual sharing and contributing, and I think we shouldn't be afraid of this.

Pastors are the facilitators or synchronizers of it all. They make sure the members of the body are loved, cared for, exercising, healthy, and moving out together at the direction of the Lord. Pastors listen to God, the chief choreographer, and then, as assistant choreographers, help place people so the work is effective . . . not necessarily efficient . . . effective.

HE MUST INCREASE, BUT I MUST DECREASE

For any ministry leader, whether paid or unpaid, full or part-time, lay or called clergy, the correct attitude must prevail. In pastoring His disciples, "Jesus called them together and said, 'You know that the rulers of the Gentiles lord it over them, and their high officials exercise authority over them. Not so with you. Instead, whoever wants to become great among you must be your servant, and whoever wants to be first must be your slave—just as the Son of Man did not come to be served, but to serve, and to give his life as a ransom for many'" (Matt. 20:25–28).

The correct attitude of all leadership is one of humility and service. Easier said than done! Many leaders in the world today are looking for fulfillment in fame, ambition, title, prestige, power, fortune, travel, connections, and possessions. But only God can satisfy us, and we had better not forget it.

Increasing seems infinitely superior to decreasing. When our ministries increase, it's wonderful. More is always better, right? When the numbers swell and we have to build, that's good news. When we have more programs, things are happening for the glory of God. Or so it seems.

> *The correct attitude of all leadership is one of humility and service.*

As we've all realized at one time or another, gauging our success on numbers isn't the end-all appraisal. What is true success? Each pastor should be able to answer that question . . . minus any discussion whatsoever about size of congregation, buildings, or programs.

Recently I did an intense study of John the Baptist. His story has stirred me deeply. It's clear he knew precisely what his calling entailed. He was the prophetic fulfillment of Isaiah 40:3–4: "A voice of one calling: 'In the wilderness prepare the way for the Lord.'" His was a strategic calling for a special moment.

John definitely worked out of this calling. Special circumstances at his birth drew the attention—and expectations—of many people. He participated in paving the way for the Messiah even while in his mother's womb, confirming for Mary the words spoken to her by the angel. John was full of the Spirit from his birth and then lived in the desert where crowds flocked to him. In every way he was made to do a specific job, and he carried it out with faithfulness, hearing people's confessions and baptizing them. He testified of the Messiah and revealed Him through Jesus' baptism.

However, in the midst of this "success," a poignant moment arrived. John's disciples came to him and said, "Rabbi, that man who was with you on the other side of the Jordan—the one you testified about—look, he is baptizing, and everyone is going to him" (John 3:26).

This was a defining moment for John. He was only in his thirties. What he was most known for during his ministry, namely baptizing, was now being eclipsed by Jesus. How would people view John now? What would happen to him? Exactly when his ministry should be increasing, would it now do exactly the opposite? Was it over for him already?

John's reply was unforgettable. He said he was full of joy that this was happening. Then he stated, "He must become greater; I must become less" (John 3:30). Wow! John was going to let it go, just like that! He was satisfied to see Jesus increase, while he decreased.

Actually, that was precisely what happened. From that moment on, John's ministry and life went downhill. The crowds lessened, and prison awaited him because of his comments regarding Herod's sin. Then there was an ignominious death, and he was gone.

None of us, however, can argue that John was not a success. He fulfilled the strategic calling given to him by God. John held his ministry lightly and let it go when it was finished, even though he was young. In fact, I believe this personal willingness to decrease so that Christ can increase is the real definition of success. Humility is indispensable.

Instead of asking about the obvious at the next ministers' meeting, I wonder what someone would say to these queries: Is it well with your soul? Is Christ being glorified more than ever in your life? Is Jesus increasing while you decrease? What is the Spirit doing that you couldn't possibly accomplish yourself? Maybe we should start asking each other some new questions.

Sometimes we forget the correct direction we are to go. Once I had a difficult situation. I had tried a number of things, but one night while I was praying about it, the Lord said to my spirit, "Carolyn, there's a barrier you've been facing. You've tried to climb over it. You've attempted to go around it. However, these haven't worked. You've forgotten that there's another direction. You can always go lower."

I took a deep breath. *"You can always go lower."* I thought and prayed about what that would look like, and then I implemented it. It was so shocking that someone involved said they didn't even know what to call it. For me it was pretty clear: it was a type of cross. Interestingly enough, the barrier was torn down within the week. Humility is the way through multiple situations.

Why put this in a chapter on the pastor? Because the church is besieged by Satan, but the way to win the victory is through humility and the cross. When these are active, the Devil backs down, God regards us and provides authority and everything we require to come out triumphant. Humbling ourselves isn't an option; it's the only way through.

Perhaps we've placed too much emphasis on leadership development in the church as a whole. I just wonder. What would happen if instead of offering a leadership course, we offered classes that focused on picking up our crosses, being obedient and giving up our desires, servanthood, humility, and accepting lowliness? Would anyone come? And would whoever came stay through the whole "training"? Wouldn't those be just the ones you would want to put into leadership? Our churches would be different if they were led by people like this. Yet, that is exactly what God intended! He pays special attention to this group. I wish we had an entire church like this. In fact, if we are the body of Christ, shouldn't His humility show up in it?

THINGS TO CONSIDER . . .

1. "A pastor's main concern should be whether or not the body—corporately and individually—is attached to Jesus, the Vine, so life can flow through, providing sustenance, energy, empowerment, and a free flow." Do you agree that this is the main task of the pastor? Do you think most pastors think of this as their main concern? If not, what would happen if they did?

2. Do we act in church as if the very presence of God is what people need and want most?

3. Pastors are meant to help keep the body of Christ healthy. What contributions does the pastor make to bring about this outcome?

4. The author talks about the importance of the pastor connecting with individuals and knowing what is going on in their lives and personal growth as Christians. How do you see this happening in your own church? What sorts of people around you (not just paid pastoral staff) have pastoral gifts?

5. What do you think about the Irish church's concept of the Holy Spirit as a wild goose? In what ways might this be an appropriate simile?

6. This chapter contains a discussion of how important it is that the maturational level be high for someone who is operating in the gifts of the Spirit. Do you agree? Why or why not?

7. What about those words of John the Baptist that Jesus must increase but he must decrease? How exactly does this apply to Christians today?

8. The author talks about the idea that we can "always go lower." How important is humility to the synchronization of the church body? Where do you see humility at work around you?

Chapter Nine

THE DIRECTIONAL PROPHETIC CURRENT

⸺⸺⸺⸺ ☙ ⸺⸺⸺⸺

Which way do we go? What do we do now? The church today is wondering what to do next. We see the massive shifts of society that hardly need to be reiterated. Amidst these changes, including huge historical shifts out of modernism and into postmodernism, how does the church not lose ground? Better yet, how does it advance?

If the church chooses to answer this question merely through human reasoning, it will most assuredly fail in its paltry attempts. Our only recourse is to let God show us what we should do next.

In Tolkien's *Lord of the Rings*, Gandalf says to Frodo, "For even the very wise cannot see all ends."[34] Although we can and should use our intelligence to consider what is happening and what might occur, this won't be enough. God Himself knows, however He's completely aware of the future and understands everything. He wants to be the chief player. He calls the moves, instead of just reacting to the Devil's scheming. If we're busy in our own smaller designs, we'll miss His bigger picture.

The kingdom of God has always been vast. As we begin to understand it, we realize that His kingdom is a much larger, more comprehensive world than our tiny individual or corporate church spheres. The directional current not only points to what direction we should go, it also pulls us away from our smaller views and shows us God's broader horizon. It increases our vista exponentially.

As we enlarge our vision and lose our myopia, we aren't content with things as they are, sensing that God desires to change them. We aren't satisfied to keep God's vision of tomorrow imprisoned by the boundary of the past nor even to the present-day ideas of what is satisfactory. God wants us to do more than just get by.

The directional current originates with an expansive vista of God and a view of the earth as His handiwork. The key is to gain His perspectives and plans. Since He is holy and righteous and in every way perfect, this current seeks to put all things into their proper places in relation to Him. It also works to correct anything that isn't as it should be. It tidies up, cleans up, washes down, props up, and puts away what shouldn't be there. Basically, it's the housecleaning crew of the church. It works to leave the church in a spotless, pure, and holy state so it can be of maximum service to the King in the work of expanding His kingdom.

Whenever I have a housecleaning crew, I pick up things so surfaces are clear to dust off and the floors are free to be washed. Picking up is my part; cleaning up is God's part. I need to get rid of the clutter and be willing to put things away. He then does the cleaning work for this current.

Why talk about housecleaning when we want to know what the church should do next? Because we can't accomplish what God desires without a thorough cleaning. So often we become concerned with what we should do when God would like us to be more concerned with obedience and godly attitudes.

First Thessalonians 5:16–22 has some clear-cut housekeeping statements: "Rejoice always, pray continually, give thanks in all circumstances; for this is God's will for you in Christ Jesus. Do not quench the Spirit. Do not treat prophecies with contempt but test them all; hold on to what is good, reject every kind of evil."

Rejoice always? Be joyful when there's nothing to be joyful about? Always? Really?

Pray continually. How? We have to live and eat and work and sleep. How can we stay on our knees all the time?

Give thanks in all circumstances. Yes, *all* circumstances, not just some of them.

Being joyful . . . praying . . . giving thanks . . . all this is God's will for us. If we follow these commands, we'll be pulled into a broader kingdom perspective, and life will look different. We'll put ourselves in the place where we can recognize and be more receptive to God's directions for us.

This passage also warns us not to put out the Spirit's fire or treat prophecies with contempt. Of course, we are to test everything so we don't swallow Satan's lies. If we discern and hold on to the good, we'll know what is of God and what isn't. As we follow the Word and "reject every kind of evil," we'll be in the place where God can use us and direct us.

Those who live any way they choose, even outside of His will, cannot expect God's direction only when they're in the mood for it. He wants to be involved in the everyday decisions of our lives, not just the big choices like where we move or what job we should have. Some people seek for prophetic direction when they aren't living clean lives (see Ezek. 14:1–11). They want a shortcut or free insurance policy, but God isn't into providing a fast track.

FOUNDATIONAL DIRECTION

In light of all this, it would be helpful to consider Ephesians 2:19–22. Here we see that the Lord wants to build a holy household. In order for this to happen, we must lay a firm and straight foundation. The church cannot miss this clarion call:

> Consequently, you are no longer foreigners and strangers, but fellow citizens with God's people and also members of his household, built on the foundation of the apostles and prophets, with Jesus Christ himself as the chief cornerstone. In him the whole building is joined together and rises to become a holy temple in the Lord. And in him you too are being built together to become a dwelling in which God lives by his Spirit.

The chief cornerstone for the church is Christ. He is the One who sets the building square. Then Scripture tells us that God uses the apostles and prophets to lay the foundation. We will see later how the apostolic work is foundational, but so is the prophetic. When these roles are firmly and properly carried out, the church will be strong and indwelt by the presence of the Lord.

Prophetic servant-leaders provide directions such as these: "No, don't lay the foundation there; that is unstable sand underneath this thin layer of dirt. Go in that direction for the foundation so it ends right there. Make this room smaller; you won't need it. Build that room larger; God wants to do a work in that area of ministry. This isn't plumbed correctly; make it straight. Build up this side; remove that hill of dirt over there and level it all out. Clean up that spot before trying to build on a trash heap. Prepare the ground in this way."

The prophets in the Bible did this directional work in many different ways. Isaiah told what to look for with the Messiah and His ministry (Isa. 53). John the Baptist was called prophetically to "make straight" the way of the Lord, including leveling out the ground (Isa. 40:3–5).

> *When prophecy is not despised, it can provide stability, firmness, confirmation, and strength.*

Those who work in the prophetic today help the church in similar ways by providing insight and direction. When prophecy is not despised, it can provide stability, firmness, confirmation, and strength. Any time God decides to share the future, the message shouldn't be scorned. He has provided that insight in order to accomplish something in particular: Perhaps to prepare God's people for coming events or to confirm that the church (or individual) is moving in the correct direction. Sometimes the Lord shares the future prophetically so that people will be warned. If we know a huge accident has happened on our highway, we can take another route. Whether a prophetic word is an affirmation or a warning, both are advantageous.

Once, someone I know was traveling and felt led to start driving in her car on a Sunday morning, feeling the Spirit would show her where she was supposed to stop and go to church. It became late and she wondered if she had missed God's direction entirely, but suddenly she saw a church ahead and felt that was the place to stop. As she sat in the service, she sensed she had a word from the Lord, but there was no space in the service for her to share it. At the end, she waited and finally felt a release to go forward and share the word with the pastor.

When she introduced herself and told him she believed she had a word from the Lord, he immediately called over the rest of the staff and deacons. As they prayed and she spoke forth the prophetic word, she noticed the pastor had tears in his eyes. At the end he revealed that during that same week, there had been two other prophetic words from outside visitors regarding precisely the same thing. Certainly it was a clear guidance from

> *The prophetic voice often speaks out to encourage people to accept change.*

the Lord about the direction the church should take.

When true prophecy from the Lord is received and not despised, it can provide confirmation, both individually and corporately. God wants to give us a straight and clear path that we can walk with confidence knowing that we are headed in the right direction. Usually a prophetic word doesn't come like a thunderbolt out of heaven when we are walking with the Lord and listening to Him. Rather, it affirms what we're already hearing from Him and strengthens us to move forward.

KEEPING IN STEP WITH THE SPIRIT

Galatians 5:25 states: "Since we live by the Spirit, let us keep in step with the Spirit." The directional current encourages the church to stay in step with the Spirit. It keeps us all moving at the same pace the Spirit is taking.

This isn't always an easy thing to discern. For the Israelites wandering through the desert, they had the pillar of cloud by day and the pillar of fire by night. When the pillar lifted, they packed up and moved. When it rested, they waited and stayed put. It might well be considered a "hurry up and wait" kind of life. This tends to be God's way.

Sometimes He says, "Now!" and then we're supposed to obey immediately. We must jump, or we have to run to keep up. There are moments when we would much prefer to think about it all for a while, but we don't have time. He needs us to act, just as when the Spirit told Philip the evangelist to rise and go south down the desert road where he amazingly intersected with the Ethiopian eunuch in one of those God encounters (Acts 8:26–40).

On the other hand, He often tells us to stop. It seems like He is languishing around, and we wonder why we can't get going.

Both of these are difficult times. In the first, we often don't feel ready for what He has asked us to do. During the waiting periods, however, the Lord wants to prepare us. He builds those traits in us that will be needed, stores up our strength, and teaches us to trust in Him. If we hurry through the holding patterns, we'll circumvent the preparation process for when He wants us to obey . . . and quickly. We must learn to be at peace in both scenarios.

The Spirit is the leading partner, and we had better comply or we run the risk of a big mess. Those who oversee the flow of this current will assist the church in understanding the Spirit's nudges and movements. They'll help us to speed up when we should, get in line, or slow down. We should be careful that we neither run ahead nor lag behind. God simply wants us to keep in step with the Spirit.

The Lord's timing is perfect. The prophetic voice often speaks out to encourage people to accept change. God wants them to be ready for what He has for them to do. Likewise, when folks are moving too quickly, the prophetic voice might recommend a bit of a slowdown. God can then work to bring more people on board or to adjust things so they better fit into the bigger picture of His kingdom work. The church is composed of a flock of sheep, and God likes to keep everyone together.

Often prophetic servants receive pictures, visions, or dreams that put things into perspective. Prophetic perspectives help us to see. Remember the "seers" who were part of the Old Testament. We gain the greater view of what will happen in the future and what our roles will entail. This is crucial to the victory of the church. It's one of the main ways we come to understand the tactics and strategies of both God and Satan. The Lord uses it so we're less likely to be deceived by the Enemy as we come into the last days. Surely this is something we need right now as we consider what the church should do next. God knows, and He wants to help us see it.

The church today is suffering from a great lack of seeing. Our eyes are dim and our understanding is less robust than it could be. Probably of all the currents, this prophetic current is the smallest. In some ways, it's a mere trickle. Ponder the strength of this current in Old Testament times and in the early church. The prophetic voices were strong, taking a crucial role in what happened to Israel and with new believers in the early church.

THE DIRECTIONAL CURRENT FOR ISRAEL

The role of the prophet in the Old Testament was jealously guarded by the Lord, who warned of false prophets. Old Testament prophets provided significant direction for the Israelites.

One place the Lord made this evident was when Saul was camped with his army at Gilgal. Samuel had anointed Saul as king and then provided him some direction. Saul would prophesy, Samuel said, and then he could "do whatever your hand finds to do." Saul was then supposed to go down to Gilgal but wait until Samuel arrived. He was explicitly told not to offer the sacrifices (1 Sam. 10:6-8). Saul did it anyway and explained that he "felt compelled" to offer the burnt offerings because the men were scattering (1 Sam. 13:1-12).

The point is not that Saul almost obeyed, but that he *didn't* obey. Waiting for six and seven-eighth days is not waiting seven. God had a perfect timing and a particular way of doing things that Saul didn't respect. He didn't follow God's clear directions.

Giving a burnt offering wasn't King Saul's proper role. As a result of his hubris and disobedience, Samuel—when he arrived shortly after the burnt offering—shared God's viewpoint about Saul's kingship, saying it wouldn't endure because the Lord had sought out someone else after His own heart (1 Sam. 13:13–14).

What a result from something that seems rather insignificant. However, it is significant to God when we do things our way or when we usurp anybody else's anointed role. The Lord wants power and decisions to be balanced. The five gifts to the church are God's, and He chooses whom He will for each one. We aren't supposed to pickpocket or shoplift anybody else's gift! We are in great need of this directional current today. We need to let the prophetic voices take their places and do what they alone are called to do.

Amos 3:7 states, "Surely the Sovereign Lord does nothing without revealing his plans to his servants the prophets." The Lord wants to provide us with guidance, direction, and encouraging confirmation. Through this current we come to understand how His Word is applied to our situation, and we have the opportunity to obey explicitly. He lets us know His impeccable timing and how He intends to move. Through provisions such as these, faith is built as we become a part of His perfect plans.

It seems to me that this current is at a trickle today because we don't often recognize who is anointed prophetically to help us know God's plans. Furthermore, we're apt to shut down the prophetic current rather than receive it as a gift from God.

As a result, we're often awash, wondering what to do next, and confused about how the Lord is about to move. Even when we think we know, the affirmation is often missing that would provide strength and faith to move ahead. Then, accompanying all of this is a shaky sense of God's timing. This leaves us all weaker than God desires, and I count it very sad.

In order for the church to step into the last days and defeat the Enemy as God intends, the Lord wants to restore the strength of this current. Certainly it is one of His five gifts to the church, and we had best not spurn it but accept it gratefully.

HE WHO HAS EARS TO HEAR

When prophetic voices speak, we have a choice: Do we want to heed them or not? Jesus said, "Whoever has ears to hear, let them hear" (Mark 4:9). Certainly we can hear something with our ears but not with our hearts. We can have someone provide us with advice but not accept it. This choice is always ours with the prophetic current.

The Spirit desires to say things to us so we will hear them and respond. He wants to see turning points. I think of Nathan, whom God sent to confront David with the sin of taking Bathsheba and having her husband killed. In the form of a story, Nathan got to the crux of the problem. Would David hear? Would he repent? As Nathan ended his story and David reacted in anger, Nathan said, "You are the man!" (2 Sam. 12:7). David didn't deny it and responded, "I have sinned against the LORD" (2 Sam. 12:13). David moved into one of those turning points.

So it is with each of us. God strives with us, yearning for us to be in right standing with Him. This is the work of all members of the Trinity as they take part in the directional current, just as they have all been integrally involved in the other currents.

For example, the Holy Spirit carries the prophetic word and delivers it through human beings. "Above all, you must understand that no prophecy of Scripture came about by the prophet's own interpretation of things. For prophecy never had its origin in the human will, but prophets, though human, spoke from God as they were carried along by the Holy Spirit" (2 Peter 1:20–21).

Again we discover that this current has its origins in God Himself. Human efforts and thinking get in the way of what God wants to accomplish as much as, perhaps more than, any of the other currents we have looked at.

God the Father knows the future and has plans and designs. He is certainly the source of this current and desires to pour it out: "I am God, and there is no other; I am God, and there is none like me. I made known the end from the beginning, from ancient times, what is still to come. I say, 'My purpose will stand, and I will do all that I please'" (Isa. 46:9–10).

God yearns for us to learn what He wants to do and to become a part of it. His purpose will stand, and He will accomplish what He intends, with or without us. However, He would rather have us come alongside His plan as we listen and obey.

Jesus was greatly involved in this current. He constantly referred to the prophets of the past and showed how He fulfilled their prophecies. Jesus shared that He had not come "to abolish the Law or the Prophets" but to fulfill them (Matt. 5:17). His birth was integrally linked to the birth of another prophet, John the Baptist. Many people referred to Jesus as a prophet. When He visited His hometown and folks didn't believe, Jesus quipped, "A prophet is not without honor except in his own town and in his own home" (Matt. 13:55).

Jesus' prophetic voice had to be recognized, and so do the prophetic voices God uses today. Though the Jews had awaited the Messiah for hundreds of years, when He came, they missed Him. They weren't able to recognize or accept His prophetic voice. Likewise, if we disregard the prophetic voices around us, there is certain deficit.

The work of the Trinity in prophecy was an integral part of the New Testament church. In 1 Corinthians 14:1 Paul wrote, "Follow the way of love and eagerly desire gifts of the Spirit, especially prophecy." Are we following this command? Do we earnestly desire that we might prophesy? It isn't meant to be an optional consideration that we engage at our convenience. Paul also wrote, "Therefore, my brothers and sisters, be eager to prophesy, and do not forbid speaking in tongues" (1 Cor. 14:39). So many people I know are less than eager to prophesy and hesitant to support those who do.

STANDING IN GOD'S COUNCIL

A prophetic voice given by God will not speak what they want to say but what the Lord has for them to share. Jeremiah 23:16–18 refers to false prophets who speak on their own:

> This is what the LORD Almighty says: "Do not listen to what the prophets are prophesying to you; they fill you with false hopes. They speak visions from their own minds, not from the mouth of the LORD. They keep saying to those who despise me, 'The LORD says: You will have peace.' And to all who follow the stubbornness of their own hearts they say, 'No harm will come to you.' But which of them has stood in the council of the LORD to see or to hear his word? Who has listened and heard his word?"

The directional current must pour out from the council room of God. This is essential. It cannot have a source anywhere else. If it does, then directions will be confusing, opposing, and incorrect. This current doesn't originate out of the wise thinking of people. Rather, it issues forth when believers take the time to stand in God's presence and learn what He has to say about things.

Imagine if this doesn't happen. Joe will have one idea and Henrietta will have another. Lois will think her solution is the best and Susanna is sure hers is. Harry is positive that his experience will take care of a problem; he wants to handle it his way. You get the picture, and you've seen it happen too.

Today this current must flow more strongly so these sorts of fleshly voices can more readily be hushed in the presence of God. They all need to come before Him in prayer and submit their human opinions to His scrutiny. They need to arrive at an understanding of what He wants to have done and when. The directional current will effectively draw believers into His council room. Everybody is invited in.

When we pay attention to God instead of hearkening to others and to societal trends, He may well set us to doing things differently. We might be required to stand up against a popular notion of our times. We could be asked to do something unusual. This current asks for us to go God's way and none other, no matter what the cost. When we have the courage to listen to God and follow His directions, the results can be astonishing.

UNPOPULAR PROPHETIC VOICES

When true prophets speak from God, they often have unpopular messages. Even as God accomplishes His purposes, attitudes can easily and quickly turn against the prophetic person. God's ways generally go contrary to the stream of worldly currents, which don't have their source in Him but in the flesh or in Satan. People often don't like the one who has a different voice and is going another direction. They get convicted and uncomfortable and want to silence the voice.

So who would want to be involved in this prophetic current? It's likely to mean unpopularity and persecution; often it has ended in death. Scripture tells us that the Pharisees were upset when Jesus went "against the flow" by healing on the Sabbath (John 5:16); forgiving sins (Luke 5:21–24); and driving out demons (Matt. 12:24).

Following Jesus means marching to a different drummer than the world does. It requires listening to His beat, His tune. When I preach and teach, I usually pray the Lord will help me to

> *Following Jesus means marching to a different drummer than the world does.*

say exactly what He wants me to—no more and no less. If He wants me to speak, I shouldn't hold back. Neither should I add anything to His message.

Although the cost of catching God's prophetic current might be pricey, Jesus said, "Blessed are you when people insult you, persecute you and falsely say all kinds of evil against you because of me. Rejoice and be glad, because great is your reward in heaven, for in the same way they persecuted the prophets who were before you" (Matt. 5:11–12).

A huge part of the main flow in this directional current is to speak out, according to God's timing. If people get offended, that is their choice. I believe the Holy Spirit always works to say things in a way that people are most likely to hear and assimilate. However, if they don't and they get angry, so be it. Whatever God wants to have said has been shared. That's the responsibility of the prophet: not to hold back what God wants to say, regardless of the price.

False prophets don't want to annoy people, so they'll say whatever makes folks happy. In order for this current to flow from God, people must be willing to declare whatever God wishes no matter what it means to their reputation or comfort. They have to love others enough to warn and correct if that is what God wants.

A popular perspective today is that any prophecy should be edifying, and so it should. This term, however, is often thought to mean "always positive." Therefore, some believe any prophetic word that is negative in any way is probably incorrect. Of course, this can't be an appropriate test. We know from Scripture that false prophets often gave positive words because they wanted the favor of the king. It was often the true prophet who had the warning of dire consequences to come and was forced to endure the king's anger.

Something is edifying when it improves the mind or the character. We can improve when we're reproved. Sometimes a word of correction is the most edifying of all.

That this is available from God is a comforting thought. If I'm doing something incorrectly, I would rather know it sooner than later, before I get into a bad habit, just as when learning to ski or some other sport or skill. God cares enough to correct us and save us a lot of hassles. Even when He has to discipline us, this is good, because the correction is helpful toward our improvement.

The prophetic word can be used to share God's correction to us individually or as a church. If the plumb line is off even a little, we can build ourselves into the leaning tower of Pisa. The Lord wants the church to be built square and straight, so He uses this important aspect of His Spirit to do that work.

If the church leadership and those who oversee this current as prophetic servants want to be popular, they will never correct or will always do it quietly with a smile. However, this is akin to my knowing a friend has cancer and furthermore being able to perform the surgery to remove it, but refusing to do so. Sin is like a cancer. It will spread if left unattended. Yes, it may take a knife to cut out the tumor, but if this isn't done, the sin will grow and death will result.

We dare not skip this highly important current in the church today. Who wants a cancerous church? We need people who will build up the church by encouraging, affirming, and also correcting. All of this is part of our housecleaning job in this current. We are called to "speak the truth in love" and to "care enough to confront."

First Corinthians 14:3 says, "But the one who prophesies speaks to people for their strengthening, encouraging and comfort."

This mighty current is meant to build a strong, holy, confident, and mature church that can move out with boldness and assurance. May the Lord help us to recognize the leaders He has developed for this current and to release them to do His bidding. The Lord has given people as gifts for the clear flowing of this housecleaning directional current. Oh, that we might be able to free up this stream!

THINGS TO CONSIDER . . .

1. Part of what happens when the prophetic current is operating properly is that we are pulled out of our smaller dimension and into God's bigger and more expansive picture. What exactly are we missing when we do not get this kind of perspective?

2. This chapter discusses the role of the prophetic voice in helping to lay the foundation for the church. It provides direction, insight, future preparation, and clean-up. In what ways is this active in your church?

3. How can the prophetic work of pointing toward the future assist in strengthening and encouraging the church? Give some examples.

4. How exactly do we keep in step with the Spirit as it exhorts us to do in Galatians 5:25?

5. "The church today is suffering under a great lack of seeing." Do you agree with this statement or not? Explain your thinking.

6. Do you believe that the prophetic gift needs to be active in these last days? How can we help it increase?

7. In 1 Corinthians 14:39 Paul says, "Therefore, my brothers and sisters, be eager to prophesy, and do not forbid speaking in tongues." Is the church following this verse today?

8. When we stand "in the council of the Lord to see or to hear his word" (Jer. 23:18), we will be able to prophesy accurately and to get along as a body. Is the prophetic current flowing strongly today directly from God's throne room?

Chapter Ten

THE PROPHETIC SERVANT

--- ☩ ---

A question people often ask me is "How do you know that a prophetic voice is from God or not?" Jesus addressed this by saying, "Watch out for false prophets. They come to you in sheep's clothing, but inwardly they are ferocious wolves. By their fruit you will recognize them. Do people pick grapes from thornbushes, or figs from thistles?" (Matt. 7:15–16).

We recognize true prophets by their fruit. This isn't the number of friends on Facebook or followers on Twitter. It is the fruit of the Spirit, which are qualities of character a person shows when outside their stage persona. Even authenticity can be faked at a podium, but true fruit will be obvious behind the scenes when the going gets rough. If the person is impatient, unloving, unkind, grumpy, demanding, self-centered, and disrespectful, Jesus says they cannot be a true prophet. Though they look like sheep while behind the microphone, they are deceptive.

Scripture often describes true prophets as being particularly humble, like Moses for example. They don't allow getting insight from the Lord to go to their heads. Using a prophetic word to control or gain power is reprehensible. If you meet so-called prophets who are pretentious and act like they have an "in" with God, lording it over others, these are not true prophets. Prophets who are sent from God won't seek to draw attention to themselves but will point to Jesus. They will acknowledge everyone in the body of Christ, showing honor and respect to other prophets and those anointed in the other four leadership gifts.

Another obvious test of a true prophet is whether what they say agrees with Scripture. God will never go against Himself. Just as Jesus came to fulfill the law and the prophets, so God fulfills and cements His Word. The Lord also fulfills the word of a true prophet. Even if at first we might think something is "out in left field," that word will ultimately come to pass. I once knew a pastor who received a word that he would be the next state leader for his denomination. He thought this was impossible, but within just a few years, this is exactly what happened, and he remembered this prophetic word, which at first he was unable to conceive was correct. God had indeed spoken it, and God fulfilled it.

In 1 John 4:1 we are told not to "believe every spirit, but [to] test the spirits to see whether they are from God, because many false prophets have gone out into the world." This passage goes on to say that you can recognize the Spirit of God when the person acknowledges Jesus as having come in the flesh. Because of this, true prophets won't mind when others test them or ask questions regarding what they believe. They are happy when other prophets have additional understanding or perspectives to share about their revelation, and they are humbly receptive to any necessary correction regarding delivery. Furthermore, they are teachable and open, not just to one or two individuals of their personal choosing but to other leaders in the body. Mature prophetic servants realize they don't "have it all." They simply want truth from God, whether He uses them or others.

Another identifier is that true prophets will be real servants. They are eager to assist and encourage. They have a great attitude, and they live holy lives. God has called them, anointed them, and given them as gifts to the church. They didn't ask for the prophetic role in order to assume a title and attention; God determined it.

True prophets stand in the council of God and speak what He wants. They don't get their words from one another or from their own minds and thinking. They're willing to spend time with the Lord and to listen to His voice. Jeremiah 23:30–32 says, "I am against the prophets who steal from one another words supposedly from me. Yes . . . I am against the prophets who wag their own tongues and yet declare, 'The LORD declares.' Indeed, I am against those who prophesy false dreams. . . . They tell them and lead my people astray with their reckless lies, yet I did not send or appoint them. They do not benefit these people in the least."

Those who are called by God and ready to be used as true prophets have gone through a process of dying to their flesh, so it doesn't get mixed up in their messages. They've been "formed" and transformed, becoming more and more like Jesus. As they follow Him closely, true prophetic servants learn what it means to take up their cross daily. If the Lord asks them to say something unpopular, they obey. They're willing to pay any price to speak what God wants, even to the place of martyrdom.

Should God give them a difficult message, they don't delight in delivering it. They're careful to understand its aspects, timing, and delivery methods, and when the moment has come, they're grieved to have to share it. They can deliver the message out of a deep love, not out of a haughty spirit. True prophets know how to pray and intercede and consistently do so.

TERMINOLOGY PROBLEMS

We have some confusion to address regarding the prophetic voice. In Matthew 24:24 Jesus warned about the last days saying, "For false messiahs and false prophets will appear and

> *If we leave a void among true prophetic servants, Satan will step into the void and fill it with false ones.*

perform great signs and miracles to deceive, if possible, even the elect. See, I have told you ahead of time." This problem will be critical enough that Jesus warned us about it.

Right now, I can see how this could happen. First of all, there's little understanding about the prophetic role in the church today. Also lacking is a good grasp of what constitutes a true prophetic servant. When people learn how to identify counterfeit money, they don't study the counterfeits—they study the details of real money. Since it would appear that there are few prophetic role models who are properly functioning and who are easily recognizable by the majority of the church today, who does one study? Where can a person receive training in what constitutes a true prophetic servant called by God as opposed to a false prophet? We have a desperate need of teachers in these areas, and they're around but seldom used.

You've probably noticed that I often use phrases other than the word *prophet*. Let me explain my reasoning. It isn't that I don't believe the prophetic voice still occurs today—quite the contrary. However, we have a problem on hand.

Quite a few false prophets have usurped the word *prophet*. When people hear the term, they associate it with wackos and craziness. A person who is called and gifted by God for the church is almost unable to associate with the term because they will be misjudged. Worst of all, no one will listen to them, even when they're delivering God's message. Wanting to have the opportunity to function properly, they forgo the phrase.

As we noted earlier, those who are false prophets show they aren't of God. They function in pride, look for power and control, haven't developed the fruit of the Spirit, and don't listen to God but speak their own words. This is why I've used the term "prophetic servant" or "prophetic voice." I want to separate the proper functioning of this role today from the false.

Also there's an idea that the prophet's role has ended, even though we can be open to prophecy. I believe that not everyone who works in prophecy as a gift of the Spirit is automatically a prophet called by God into the leadership role and gifting that oversees the directional current for the church. They can simply be members of the body of Christ who are ministering to others through the prophetic. Yes, they're part of the current, but they aren't necessarily gifted by God to be leaders in the current. Another way of putting this is that all prophets prophesy, but not all who prophesy are prophets given to the oversight of this current. That is God's selection, and His alone.

Some believe that the prophet's role has ceased. I don't see evidence of this in Scripture. Certainly prophecy continues. Furthermore, Ephesians 4 clearly states that prophets are supposed to be one of the five leadership gifts to the church. Some say it is over because there is no evidence in the New Testament of passing on the prophet's office, but neither is there for an evangelist.

I'm not here to quibble. If we get hung up on these sorts of things and stop at this titling issue, we'll lose sight of the real need. This is where much of the Pentecostal and Charismatic church finds itself today. I don't care what we call them, there are certainly men and women anointed by God today to serve in the role of overseeing the directional, prophetic current of the church. If we don't understand this and fail to cultivate these roles, we'll suffer the great loss of one of Christ's dearly purchased gifts to the church. This role is also meant to serve as the foundational base, along with the apostles. Losing the base, well, it's almost inconceivable! If we leave a void among true prophetic servants, Satan will step into the void and fill it with false ones. How we need to turn this thing around!

THE ICEBERGS

I always say that a true prophetic servant will be like an iceberg: 90 percent under the water and 10 percent out. A prophetic overseer can often be discovered in the ranks of your church's prayer warriors and intercessors—the hidden portion of the iceberg.

Remember that the directional current flows from standing in the council room of God. It's impossible to be a true prophet and not spend time with the Lord in prayer. Scripture tells us that God shares His plans with the prophets first. However, it doesn't necessarily follow that they should share His plans and concerns with others . . . at least not right away. The first task is to pray about it. As the prophetic servants spend time with the Lord regarding what He has showed them, the issue will gain clarity and perspective. It will deepen until they come to sense the heart of the Lord for that situation.

Often they'll be moved into intercession. In this kind of prayer, there's a gap that stands between God and the individual, church, group, organization, state, or nation. One of the main roles of prophetic overseers is to grasp God's hand while simultaneously holding on to the situation. They must keep this posture until the two pull together. This is often ripping, strenuous, and difficult work. It may mean tears, cries of agony, or moans because a true intercessor doesn't just feel the pain in theory. Many times the prophetic voice is never heard because the prophet has been faithful to speak to God, who has changed things. The situation is cleared up without anything being said.

True prophets do the work of noting the breaks in the wall of defense and going to the gap to repair them (Ezek. 13:3–5).

They are the watchmen on the wall who blow the trumpet to warn of an advancing enemy (Ex. 33:1–11).

The church needs to know who these people are and appreciate their efforts. These intercessors are a definite part of the prophetic movement. Again, like those being used in prophecy as a gift of the Spirit, not all intercessors are automatically prophetic voices, but people with prophetic voices are generally intercessors and can be found in the prayer ranks.

The work that prophetic servants often do in their "90 percent under" status sometimes causes them to feel out of sync. As they're greatly burdened and intercede for changes they feel God wants, they're often in a lamenting stage while others are in a laughing stage. While others are enjoying their sin, the prophetic servants are weeping over it. However, when those folks finally repent and are crying at the altar, those operating in the prophetic are smiling and happy.

This can be more difficult than it seems. It's probably why prophets in the Old Testament wore sackcloth and sat in ashes. A scratchy cloth under your clothes and next to your skin can help a person bear with some rebellious, partying, sinful matters in the world while the prophet's spirit is simultaneously deeply grieved. The scratchiness brings the outward "fluff" into harmony with one's heavy, prophetic spirit. That's probably hard to understand in our contemporary society, but perhaps this is because we need more people who are in sync with God's viewpoint instead of being in sync with the world's perspective.

Often prophetic servants experience a sort of "holy discontent." This may be born in quiet for a time, but more often than not the Spirit ultimately wants to unveil it and use it to point out the changes He desires in a church or individual, an organization or group. I suppose this could seem like a bad or critical attitude in the prophetic person (and if it's carnal, it is), but if the discontent is given by the Lord, one should hearken

> *God owns the space in a church service; it isn't ours to commandeer.*

to it. During time spent in prayer, God will prepare the prophetic servants to speak out a call to change. The Lord will help them to deliver the message in the best way possible so it will most likely be accepted.

As prophetic overseers pray, they come to discern and respect God's timing and methods. They don't jump to share what God has showed them but rather pray for the correct timing. They allow God to arrange circumstances and open up the hearts of people to receive. When it's the right moment and the Lord has arranged the events, they share God's message.

During this time of prayer and intercession, prophetic servants are often changed. They may be broken, convicted of their own part, repent, and humble themselves. Love for the people is poured out by the Lord so there's grief rather than haughtiness when correction is part of the message. Their attitudes are cleared up, and their own ideas are removed. In short, they're prepared to be a clean vessel through whom God can work.

Isaiah said, "The Sovereign Lord has given me a well-instructed tongue, to know the word that sustains the weary" (Isa. 50:4). The Lord cares about communicating His message clearly, and He has a response in mind. The prophetic servant senses what this response should be and is in pain if that response doesn't occur. It's so hard to deliver a carefully prepared message from the Lord and have it either spurned or ignored. One feels the sorrow in the heart of the Father. This happens as well when the timing for a word is here but no space is allowed for it to be delivered.

God owns the space in a church service; it isn't ours to commandeer. He has priorities and plans. When there's no space left for

Him to enter in, it defeats our desire of honoring the presence and activity of the Lord in our midst. When song follows closely upon song and then the offering and sermon, things can be so tightly compacted that the Spirit of God doesn't have room to move, and oh, how we need the breath of the Spirit!

THE PROPHETIC TOOLBOX

God has provided the prophetic servant with a huge toolbox. The problem is, some aren't aware of it. They tend to do or even say the same thing over and over in an unvaried way. A typical approach is the formalized one: "Thus saith the Lord" . . . with the message then delivered in a somewhat stilted vocal tone.

Although noting that the Lord is about to speak is a viable method at times, it's not the only way. There are many informal approaches that I believe He would also like to use.

When a person pastors, for example, they don't announce, "Lo! I'm now going to pastor you." They just do it. This is true in relationship to prophetic words and acts as well.

When a prophetic voice needs to be heard, if individuals are listening, they'll hear and recognize it. So often I've been in a situation when a word from the Lord has been given, but the prophetic servant did it in their normal voice and tone. Even though things seemed as usual, my heart was quickened, and I knew instantly it was from the Lord. Sometimes there are even tears or other emotional reactions because the person delivering the message is "being carried along by the Spirit" (2 Peter 1:21), and He is at work.

God has particular methods and places by which His message is best given. There are so many considerations. Are others around? Should they be or not? How many and who should be included in the word? How should it be given? Loudly, whispered, sternly, happily? What is the proper tone? Which of the

> *The mouth of the prophetic servant must be under the care and restraint of the Spirit.*

many methods possible does God wish to use? How firmly should the message be delivered? These are all aspects the prophetic person needs to consider.

The strength with which the Lord wants to give forth His word is an important point to discern. It's inappropriate to select a hammer out of the prophetic toolbox if God wants to use the tweezers. Hammers slam and smash; tweezers gently extract.

By the loudness and tone of their voices, prophetic servants sometimes select a hammer when they weren't meant to do that. God doesn't want to smash someone to smithereens. His message gets stronger as a person or church continues to disobey, just like we do in parenting. We might start with a gentle word, but if the child disobeys, we get increasingly more definitive and stern. God starts in the same way, and if we listen, great. A difficult and strongly corrective word should always be followed up with an opportunity for restoration.

At times a prophetic word may be sensed in its completeness by prophets, but that doesn't automatically mean they are to deliver the whole message—at least not all at once. It would be too much. There are times when I've preached, and in the Spirit I've sensed a block from the people regarding a particular concern. Sometimes I speak regarding the issue for a little while, sort of leaning against the block. When they won't budge, I sense the Lord taking a step back so He can come at it again another time when they're more open.

If, on the other hand, the receivers of the word are tender and sensitive, not much will have to be said before they repent and obey. Only a little drill bit is needed. How wonderful it is to preach to such a group and just by suggesting an issue and pointing the way out of it, they immediately respond. One can keep talking, sharing truth, going deeper, and a radical and profound transformation can occur through the Holy Spirit.

So in all of these cases the prophetic servants must sense how much needs to be said, when, and in what manner. Under the power of the Holy Spirit, they'll have the guidance they need, but they should never try to trump God and deliver the message their way or even in the same way every time. Each situation is different.

This includes another aspect that can be difficult for a prophetic voice. If the person tends to chatter too much with their own personal ideas, then the voice of God won't be easily distinguished. The mouth of the prophetic servant must be under the care and restraint of the Spirit. They must learn to listen a lot, both to others and to God. Out of the depths of this unseen core of being, God is able to rise up and make Himself known when and as He chooses.

A WIDE VARIETY

God uses distinctive methods to deliver His prophetic word for different situations. Sometimes a word is supposed to be delivered in a church service or perhaps afterwards or before or some other day of the week. At times the message is for an individual, or a small group, or the leaders, or the whole church. The word might be given over a dinner table, at the altar, in the foyer, over the phone, through a written note, or orally. It might be delivered in a committee meeting when the prophetic person sees an answer or provides direction that is clearly from the Lord.

Prophetic words can be in a teaching or in a sermon, although not all sermons are automatically prophetic words. At times, preaching is God's chosen way to move people to the place they need to be as a church. Things can shift in the spiritual realm as God's messages are delivered and allowed to take root in the hearts of the people. This is all part of the functioning of the prophetic servant.

I've known pastors who have preached for a while on a certain topic. The people's hearts were prepared. The church invited a prophetic servant to speak who knew nothing of the subject at hand. Then that person spoke forth the same theme, and there was a sudden and permanent shift in the church. The words of the prophetic servant brought things into being because they were prophetic words from God, and when the Lord speaks, things happen.

In Genesis God spoke the earth, and all its aspects, into existence. Speaking forth God's word by the Holy Spirit can bring change, growth, and life. Things move into place that weren't present before. Remember, these changes don't happen because of the personal ability of the prophetic person but entirely because of the power of God and His word.

Throughout Scripture we see prophetic words delivered in a wide variety of ways. Sometimes the prophet shared a story that got the point across, such as Nathan with David. At other times God asked them to perform a symbolic act, as Jeremiah and the linen belt (Jer. 13) and Agabus binding his own hands (Acts 21:10–11). The Lord might give a "picture" that succinctly explains a situation and what He wants to do about it, just as Jesus did with His parables. This and other uses of simile and metaphor can help us to understand God's bigger design. He also uses dreams and visions to show what is to come (e.g., Joseph) or to help us understand what is happening (like Peter's vision before meeting Cornelius).

Each of these methods is proper only in its correct place as God chooses to use it. We should never seek these methods for themselves. We aren't to seek after visions for their own sake or any other kind of demonstration of the Spirit for that matter. We seek God Himself, not the experiences.

Prophetic servants may often be found in the ranks of administration. Consider Isaiah, for example, who was a scribe for King Uzziah (2 Chron. 26:22) and served through four kings of Judah (Isa. 1:1). He was involved in political aspects and the government of the nation, but think of his valuable assistance if he could last through four different reigns—something almost unheard of today. His excellent administrative assistance and relationships gave him direct access to speak prophetically. How useful that prophetic direction apparently became to the kings.

Many times the Lord places His prophetic servants in roles of potential influence where they can come to the table and where their prophetic voice can be heard as God chooses. They know what is happening in the inner workings and can be a part of the decision-making processes. In this way, God assures that His voice can be heard.

As one learns the various means by which the prophetic current is released, we realize it can be all around us. Many times we're unaware just how God is working in this current.

At times the prophetic ministry is coupled with one or more of the spiritual gifts. This might include a word of knowledge, a word of wisdom, discernment, or faith. For example, God may show a prophetic servant something that person wouldn't normally know, for example, that the person's son is running away from God. This would, of course, be a word of knowledge. Under the inspiration of the Holy Spirit, a gift of supernatural faith arises and a prophetic word is given that brings hope. In another situation of the gifts working together, a word of knowledge might indicate sin. Then a prophetic word goes forth seeking to correct and bring restoration.

Prophecy and moving in all the gifts of the Spirit, like we're discussing, was strong in the historical Irish church. Again we can see another current flowing strongly during that time period.

Adomnan, the ninth abbot of Iona, wrote a biography on Iona's founder, Columba (AD 521–597). One whole section is given over to examples of prophetic words and their outcomes. Here is one I selected. St. Columba is the one here referred to as "the blessed man," and the one referred to as "Columb" is the name of the repentant man he helped. Note how the gifts of the Spirit are at work:

> About the same time, Conall, bishop of Culerathin . . . collected almost countless presents from the people . . . to give a hospitable reception to the blessed man.
>
> Many of these presents from the people were laid out in the paved court of the monastery, that the holy "man" might bless them on his arrival; and as he was giving the blessing he specially pointed out one present, the gift of a wealthy man. "The mercy of God," said he, "attendeth the man who gave this, for his charity to the poor and his munificence." Then he pointed out another of the many gifts, and said: "Of this wise and avaricious man's offering, I cannot partake until he repent sincerely of his sin of avarice." Now this saying was quickly circulated among the crowd, and soon reaching the ears of Columb, son of Aid, his conscience reproached him; and he ran immediately to the saint, and on bended knees repented of his sin, promising to forsake his former greedy habits, and to be liberal ever after, with amendment of life. The saint bade him rise: and from that moment he was cured of the fault of greediness, for he was truly a wise man, as was revealed to the saint through that present.[35]

The Holy Spirit desires to flow fully and freely, working through prophecy and gifts of the Spirit to do His convicting work. He is the Paraclete, the One who comes alongside to help.

WHERE ARE THEY TODAY?

Where are those who are called out to oversee this current today? They're probably hiding! Moving in the prophetic seems risky. What if they say the wrong thing? That's serious stuff, and so many worry about it. The prophetic servants sometimes fret over how people will respond to what is shared. If the word from the Lord contains a warning or correction, there may be a personal price to pay. Add to these concerns the general unpopularity and misunderstanding of the prophetic and is anyone surprised that no one wants to take this role?

Another reason not many mature prophetic servants function today is that those called literally don't know how to do it. There are some well-meaning souls who've been called, and they're trying to obey and do what God wants. Often, however, they work unwisely or inappropriately. Unfortunately, they haven't had many, if any, good role models, and furthermore they have generally had no training.

We train for evangelism; we train teachers; we certainly train pastors and missionaries. When it comes to the prophetic, however, training is clearly lacking.

To encourage budding prophetic servants and get them on the right track, challenge them to carry out a thorough study of the Scripture. Help them with useful commentaries and Bible-study supports if they need it. Suggest that they look up every single passage in Scripture that has to do with prophet, prophesy, or prophecy. They should study both the verses and the context. Then they should investigate the life of every single prophet in the bible. Among other things, this will help them to understand both the allowed variances and the essential requirements for this role. Yes, by experience I realize this is quite an undertaking, but it is worth it.

The Word and the Holy Spirit provide the best teaching for the prophetic servant. However, those who are beginning must be noted, encouraged, assisted, and nurtured so they become all God wants them to be. Ideally, mature prophetic servants should take them under their wings or at least provide loving instruction.

Let's dust off our memories: Remember when the prophetic was a staple of our heritage? Remember when we had the faith to believe there could be true prophetic ministry, and we would be given the power to discern if it weren't? Remember when we thrilled over the following verse: "Your sons and daughters will prophesy, your old men will dream dreams, your young men will see visions. Even on my servants, both men and women, I will pour out my Spirit in those days" (Joel 2:28–29).

Oh, I think we like to hear this verse quoted, but to think of it really happening? Would we truly have room in our churches for a fresh move of God as on the day of Pentecost? Would we be open to such strength and power? I think this is exactly what God wants to do. Are we ready?

As the prophetic servants are released, I believe we'll see a shift in our churches. God wants us to become counter-cultural, while presently we're more concerned with becoming pro-cultural. He has in mind for us to be change agents, while we're presently allowing the world to change us. He wants us to enjoy a life of accountability, depth, guidance, connection, and growth, while we're loving our quiet ponds and sipping our lemonades. May the Lord pour out His Spirit and equip us to be His voice in this world today.

THINGS TO CONSIDER...

1. What do you recognize as some of the characteristics of a true prophet and a false prophet? The author provides a few ideas. Do you agree? What can you add to this list?

2. How have false prophetic voices confused the issue of having people who are speaking true prophetic words?

3. In what ways should a prophetic servant of God be like an iceberg?

4. What does the toolbox of the prophetic person entail? How have you seen these tools used?

5. What budding prophetic voices do you see around you and how might those be cultivated and taught?

6. The author states that "as the prophetic servants are released, we will see a shift in our churches. God wants us to become counter-cultural while presently we are more concerned with becoming pro-cultural." What do you think is lacking in the church that prevents the prophetic current from flowing as it should?

7. On the flip side, what would our church look like if the prophetic current were flowing strongly?

8. Who do you see around you who are part of God's prophetic current?

Chapter Eleven

THE MIRACULOUS SENDING CURRENT

T he Hebrew word *shaliach* is the Hebraic equivalent of the Greek word for "apostle," which literally means "sent one." The *shaliach* was an ambassador, agent, or emissary. It was a Torah legal term for a person who was empowered by someone else to act on his behalf.

The first use of the word in the Old Testament referred to Eliezer, the servant of Abraham, who was commissioned to find a suitable wife for Abraham's son Isaac from among his own people. Legally, the *shaliach* was authorized to act on behalf of the sender. It's as if Eliezer were Abraham, having power to do whatever Abraham could do.

As such, the *shaliach* didn't give up their own personality, style, intellect, resourcefulness, creativity, and choice but used them freely on behalf of the one represented.

Another example is Moses. Exodus 7:1 tells us, "Then the LORD said to Moses, 'See, I have made you like God to Pharaoh, and your brother Aaron will be your prophet.'" This isn't at all to be misunderstood as saying that Moses was God, but rather he would be like God, a representative of God. Later in Exodus 7:7, God gave Moses directions regarding the miracles he would perform in front of the Egyptians. Moses was legally as God to Pharaoh and was given the power and authority to perform miracles and signs.

The ancient prophets were considered as *shaliachs*, sent ones. They were commissioned to deliver a message, and God had certain purposes He wanted to accomplish. God clearly "sent" Isaiah (Isa. 6:8), Jeremiah (Jer. 1:7), Ezekiel (Ezek. 3:5), and Malachi (Mal. 4:5). These were given authority to speak, backed up by miracles.

To the Jewish mind, the *shaliach* was the agent or representative, and therefore the *shaliach* was to be considered just as if he were the one who had sent him. Anything that Moses or any of the prophets did would be regarded as if it were God Himself. This explains on an even deeper level why it was so important for Moses not to strike the rock when God told him to speak to it. God was associated so closely with Moses that when Moses showed unrestrained frustration or anger with a strike, this was representative of God Himself. When anyone is this closely identified with God, obedience is absolutely necessary. We must all be aware of this as we serve Him, since we, too, are His representatives.

THE SENDING TRIUNE GOD

As we've discovered with the previous four currents, every member of the Trinity is integrally involved in each current. This is also true of the sending current, which the apostolic emissary oversees.

First of all, the Messiah Himself said that He was a "sent one" who was given authority to speak and do miracles in the Father's name: "For I did not speak on my own, but the Father who *sent me* commanded me to say all that I have spoken. I know that his command leads to eternal life. So whatever I say is just what the Father has told me to say" (John 12:49–50, emphasis mine).

> *The Lord likewise wants to send us out into some risky and potentially precarious enterprises.*

God the Father certainly sent His only Son. Anything the Son did should be regarded as though the Father did it. This is why if we don't honor the Son, we don't honor the Father, and anyone who has seen the Son, has seen the Father. When we don't love and honor the One God sent, we don't love the One who sent Him.

Secondly, both Jesus and the Father are the senders of the Holy Spirit. Note Luke 24:49 and John 14:26 and 16:7 to see that both the Father and the Son are involved in sending the Spirit. In turn, the Holy Spirit and Jesus empower and send believers.

This beautiful, mutual sending shows the heart of God for the church to push out beyond its four walls. The miraculous sending current calls us out of our comfort zones and prods us out of our no-risk lives. It asks us to be daring, to go, to be on pilgrimage, to try something new and different as God asks us.

Note that last sentence: "As God asks us." We aren't out to be risky, weird, strange, and different just for their own sakes—quite the contrary. God asks us to step out and try something daring that *He* requests of us.

The care that each member of the Trinity takes to obey and respond to each other is rarely discussed but is so important to their unity and functioning. Jesus had to obey His Father and be sent to the cross. It must have seemed terribly risky. Jesus would have to descend into the grave and go into hell. What would happen? It had never been done before. Would He win this horrendous battle by Himself? He would be cut off from the Father and from the Spirit because of the sin that was heaped upon Him.

Could He bear this? No wonder He sweat drops of blood and asked if this cup could pass from Him. Now that I have come to appreciate the working together of the Trinity, the separation must have been downright ripping! Out of this perilous endeavor to sacrifice Himself to forgive our sins, Jesus emerged victorious.

The Lord likewise wants to send us out into some risky and potentially precarious enterprises. He asks us to do it all the time, I believe, but we ignore Him. We think it doesn't make sense or we aren't sure we're hearing correctly. Sometimes we're simply afraid and unsure of ourselves. I wonder how often we've not obeyed the sending voice. I remember one time quite vividly.

I was driving to work on a normal, sunny day. Most often I selected a route through a raunchy area of town so I could pray for it. As I was driving through the area one Monday morning, I noticed a black-suited, middle-aged man with his briefcase at his side standing in front of a run-down strip mall. He seemed strangely out of place, and I naturally took note. As I did, the Holy Spirit spoke to me. "Stop and talk with him."

I would like to say that I did this immediately, but that wasn't the case. I wasn't sure it was the Lord so I just kept driving. The Lord didn't tell me why I should stop or give me a message to share. Finally, I was about four blocks away when the Spirit said, "So, you're going to be disobedient, are you?"

Oooh! Ouch! I turned my car around immediately. When I got out of the car, the man was talking on his cell phone. I waited and waited, and this wasn't a good thing to do on such a street corner, if you get my drift. It took so long, I said to the Lord, "Was this just a test of my obedience? Can I go now?"

The Spirit said, "No, he wouldn't have been on his phone if you had stopped when I first asked you to." Hmmm. I waited and still had no idea what I was going to say. It was definitely awkward.

Finally the man got off the phone, and I went up to him and said something pretty dumb. "Hi. My name is Carolyn, and . . . I was driving to work this morning and felt God wanted me to stop and talk with you."

He said, "What did the Lord tell you to tell me?"

I felt like saying, "Nothing . . . all right??!!" But I didn't. However, I had noticed something. Did you pick it up too? I had said "*God* wanted me to stop," and he had said, "What did *the Lord* tell you to tell me?"

I came back with, "You said 'the Lord.' So you're a Christian, then?"

"Aaahhh . . . umm . . . yeah!" he mumbled. Now I could understand a yes or no . . . but the hesitation? What was that about? I stood by.

He shook his head and lowered it. "I can't believe you came today."

Well, I still didn't know what this was about, but I knew I had the right day!

The man went on to explain that he was a backslidden Christian. He had gotten fed up with the church, and he had left his wife and three kids back east out of frustration and moved to Minnesota. He met a woman and "shacked up with her," he told me, even though he "knew it was wrong." He poured out his heart, and I listened. He had tried breaking up with the woman, but she kept calling him. She had found a house and wanted him to go in with her and buy it. That afternoon was the time to sign the papers! He ended his story by repeating, "I can't believe you stopped today."

Of course, I had a few things to share in return. I'm not ordained for nothing so I shared how sin always bogs us down and leads to unhappiness and death. I told him that God loved

> *The purpose of the sending/missional current is to get us out: out of our churches, out of our boxes, out of our safe places.*

him and wanted to save him from this misery. I don't remember the rest, but he was weeping. "Sir," I said, "let's pray together. You start."

"I can't," he breathed in sharply. "I haven't prayed for a long time."

"And that's exactly why you need to be the one to pray," I said. I wanted him and God to get on speaking terms again. He did pray . . . asking the Lord to forgive him. I prayed too. I had a picture of him kneeling down by the bed next to his wife, and I felt sure the Lord wanted to heal and restore their marriage. I told the man about it. Then I asked him, "What are you going to do now?"

"Well," he answered, "I'm going to call my wife, and I'm certainly not going to sign the papers on that house this afternoon!" With that assurance, I left him with some follow-up contacts.

Now I'm not particularly proud of this story. Do you know why? I came very close to not making this connection at all. I was driving in the other direction and nearly didn't stop. God was looking for a *shaliach* to represent Him in reaching this man; God wanted me to be that representative. What would have happened to that man if I had not listened to that still, small voice, or avoided it because I was afraid?

This experience changed my sending mentality. I'll go anywhere and try anything when God tells me to do so. If I make a fool of myself, what does it matter? People's lives are hanging in the balance.

GET OUT

The purpose of the sending/missional current is to get us out: out of our churches, out of our boxes, out of our safe places. God wants us to get out into our communities. Out of our denominational boundaries. Out of our racial and gender barriers. Out of our cultural habits. Out of our age delineations. Out of our everyday, boring agendas. Out of our region. Out of our country. Out of our economic class.

John 3:16 says, "For God so loved the world that he gave his one and only Son. . . ." He loves the whole world, not just our part of it. He sent Jesus cross-culturally. Christ is beyond time and gender and every single wall and line that keeps us from each other. He has crossed all the barriers, and this current asks us to do the same. Our human tendency is to conceptualize Jesus "like us." We want Him to identify with us on our terms, instead of us identifying with Him on His terms. Jesus calls us to cross the lines and go out.

This sending current is different in many ways from the wooing current, although they certainly flow close to one another. Evangelists can function within their own territories and with people to whom they can easily relate. Getting outside of their present world isn't a prerequisite to their functioning. After all, there are people who need Christ all around us.

The sending current, however, always sends . . . always moves forth! It goes outside the normal zone. If we didn't have this current, the local church would get stuck within its own parameters. It would incline toward selfishness, lack of holistic perspective, and internal stagnation. As much as each and every individual has to expand their horizons, the local church also has to extend in order to be healthy. The kingdom of God is so much greater than any single, individual church.

One way a church can do this is to send out missionaries. This term is derived from the Latin counterpart of the word for apostle—*missio* (sent away, on a mission).

A one-time financial gift or visit isn't all it takes to pull the church into the new culture where the missionaries are serving. To transport the church out of itself takes continued connections with the missionaries, reports, and prayers for them. When missionaries visit a church, there should be time to discuss the reality of the missionary efforts, the challenges, and the needs. People must connect to the work of God beyond themselves. Even going on a mission trip is a help toward this end, because people see with their own eyes and receive a true burden to help others.

Many churches consider their main goal in relation to missionaries to be financial support. Once this can be assured, they don't think they need to do anything else. The missionaries, however, have something to give back, and that is to link the people in the sending church to concerns outside of themselves. When they visit, missionaries should have enough time to share about their field's culture and needs, but especially to give testimonies so the people can see what God is doing. They also should explain how the local church can pray for that country and lead the people in specific intercession. Relationships can be forged with the missionaries but also with individuals in the other country as reports are shared. This is a gift to the church—it's part of developing their sending vision.

Home missionaries should be included. Sometimes we think there's a distinction between home and foreign missionaries, but huge numbers of people groups are unreached here in the US also. Home missionaries often have difficult tasks that require special sensitivity and support. Again, the local church should be aware of the needs of the special groups around them such as ethnic groups and religions, the deaf, and college students to name just a few. Those who work in chaplaincies in the hospitals and military can be important connectors.

Also, those who serve in pregnancy crisis centers, homes for battered women, orphanages and foster care, Teen Challenge and other such addiction care facilities, pro-life clinics, sex trafficking ministries such as Project Rescue, feeding the hungry, working with the poor, prison ministry, helping the aged and those with disabilities, and so many others are part of this sending current. The more we open the eyes of the church to special concerns all around us, the greater will be the flow of God's sending current.

Jesus, the One we follow, was sent to earth to be involved in an expansive worldview. The prophecy that Isaiah gave regarding the Messiah in Isaiah 42 shows that He was to "bring justice to the nations" (v. 1). He would care about all kinds of people and be sensitive to their needs: "A bruised reed he will not break, and a smoldering wick he will not snuff out" (v. 3).

Jesus went into Samaria, which others avoided; and He interacted with Mary Magdalene. He talked with the rich and the poor, the titled and those who were not, the religious leaders and the sinners, the adults and the children. The sending current that gets us out of our own affairs is not an option for the church but rather is at the core of God's own heart.

THE SENDING CURRENT

The sending current needs to flow out of each and every church and individual. Some advocate for 50 percent of a church budget being missional in nature. That would help us get the right emphasis

Again, this requires—as does every current—a listening obedience that emanates from the presence and direction of God. It isn't our responsibility to fill up our plates with do-gooder activities so we can feel better about ourselves. Rather, as individuals and as church bodies, we go forth at His behest and clear direction to do exactly and precisely what He wants us to do—no more and no less.

When we follow Him in this way, doing only what He asks of us, we will never be overworked and run down. We won't become so exhausted that we can't find time to spend with Him. We must listen to God and then get rid of every single activity on our plate that He doesn't tell us to get involved with. After that, we'll have time to do what He wants. He may ask us to stop and knock at the door of a house we've never entered before. He may nudge us to ask a harried mother if she wants prayer while we're in line at the post office. Maybe we need to bring somebody groceries. Whatever it is, just do it.

Our sending God has so much He wants us to experience. He wants us to go here and there, not just programmatically but according to His directions. This is what the sending current is all about. We all need to learn to listen to His voice and respond to the needs when we meet them. Be givers of money and time. Offer a cup of cold water.

HISTORICAL SENDING

Examples exist throughout history where the sending current flowed very strongly, such as Count Zinzendorf and the Moravian missionary movement in the 1700s and Wycliffe and the Lollards in the mid-fourteenth century. Such movements can be encouraging to us because we know that as people followed God's sending current, some wonderful results occurred. We can learn from them how to open up the flow.

One of the greatest apostolic movements in history was started by Saint Patrick, who also paid a price. This fifth-century church leader was probably born in Wales of a Roman father and a Welsh mother. He was captured by Irish raiders when he was sixteen and taken to the west coast of Ireland where he was forced to be a slave.

Although he didn't start this ordeal as a strong Christian by any means, Patrick soon became one. According to his biographical *Confession*,[36] he found himself turning to God and saying hundreds of prayers day and night. Patrick received a vision that he should walk east where he would find a boat that would take him away. He set out walking across the country and somehow managed to get to the east coast without being recaptured. The ship was there, too, and after a circuitous route, he finally got home. Now it would seem logical that Patrick would stay home, thinking he had experienced enough adventure.

He set out again, however, and went to a seminary on the European continent where he had a vision of the Irish people calling him back to Ireland. Now I ask you. Would you return to a country of people who had raided your home, captured you, taken you to their foreign land as a slave, and would want to put you back into slavery the minute they saw you? Most of us would reasonably avoid this whole endeavor.

Patrick, however, decided to obey God and go back to share the gospel. He's called "the apostle of Ireland" for a reason. When Patrick started his ministry, there was little significant Christian witness. Within his lifetime, he planted around 700 new churches, the faith was preached throughout the country, even in distant parts, and between thirty to forty (or more) of Ireland's 150 tribes became substantially Christian.[37] He baptized thousands; some say as many as 100,000.[38]

Patrick encouraged hundreds to become priests, and the *Annals of the Four Masters* say perhaps as many as 1,000 followed his leading.[39] For their training, he founded monasteries, thus developing a native clergy. He personally wrote out with his own hand 365 copies of the abgitorium (a kind of clergy manual) so they would have instructions.

One of the greatest areas that Patrick modeled was that he worked in miracles, signs, and wonders on a regular basis. He stood up to the Celtic high king and boldly went against one of his unfair decrees. Through a miracle, God saw to it that Patrick came out the victor in this famous standoff on the Hill of Slane. The darkness was pushed back in the offensive and people came to Christ.

What should always accompany true apostolic emissaries are signs and miracles, which provide evidence that they are sent from God. Such wonders also prove to unbelievers that the one true God is greater in every way from the god(s) they presently serve. Patrick and the saints who came after him in Ireland had spent time in prayer and were ready for the spiritual encounters. Numerous stories exist of their moving in the gifts of the Spirit and in mighty deeds of faith. We can take note that the active, miraculous work of God across Ireland resulted in almost an entire nation shifting from paganism to Christianity in one person's lifetime.

The model of church planting utilized was also effective. It was a team effort. The evangelistic outreach took believers into unreached territory where churches were started. Often this was instigated because someone was healed, and people believed as a result. Patrick would then leave a newly converted and maturing local team along with some of his own traveling team to pastor and teach the new family of disciples. He would move on with the rest of the team to do this all over again, taking some of the new converts with him. He thus built the sending current into the DNA of the Irish church.

The Irish church-plants became strong and healthy with local overseers who continued to make Jesus famous in their region. The abbots and not the bishops were given the highest authority in their own territory, thus keeping the leadership localized and indigenous. The monastic schools assisted in the discipleship and formation of believers, thereby contributing to a strong church. Patrick spurred an incredible apostolic movement.

After Patrick's death, the Irish participated with God in an even greater expansion of the monasteries and a spreading of the gospel that spanned the next few centuries. Education was never separated from sharing the good news; they were woven together. Pilgrim priests from Ireland were some of the first missionaries and teachers to the barbarous tribes throughout Europe.

These historic events remind us that the miraculous sending current has to flow strongly all of the time. We dare not hole up in our private little worlds. God wants us to move out, to expand His kingdom, to push back the darkness, to work in signs and wonders, and to be willing to pay any price to do His will. Every time He wants to send us—whether as an individual or as a church—we have to go. God has worked mightily before, and He can do it again . . . if we will not hold back.

THINGS TO CONSIDER . . .

1. What is a *shaliach*? Is there an equivalent of this today?

2. This chapter talks about the importance of moving out as God sends us and of being willing to risk in order to obey Him. What examples do you see of this? Where is the line where people themselves just do something whacky? Is it possible to confuse these two things?

3. Give examples of the "sending out" work of the Trinity. What would have happened if God had not sent His Son?

4. What types of people are part of the sending current? Give examples of what they're doing, where they're going, and the outcomes.

5. Discuss some of the historical movements that have come from people following our sending God. Try to include other situations you know of that weren't covered in this chapter.

6. The author discusses a time when she stepped out and went where God wanted her to go. What examples do you have of following the "sending current" wherever it went?

Chapter Twelve

THE APOSTOLIC EMISSARY

The term *apostle* is derived from the Greek word *apostolos*. The *apo* section of the word means "from" and the rest is derived from the word *stellein*, which means "to send." The word, therefore, literally means "to send away from." The "from" also denotes the authority transmitted from the sender to the one being sent.

In the Bible, the word *apostle* referred to people who were messengers, envoys, ambassadors, emissaries, or delegates. It was someone commissioned by another to represent that person in some way. The *apostolos* was sent forth with orders and with the delegated authority to complete a task on the other's behalf. There are eighty occurrences of this word and its cognates in the New Testament. The term was used interchangeably for the twelve disciples of Jesus (Matt.10:2; Mark 3:14 and 6:30; Luke 9:10 and 17: 1, 5, and 22:14 and 24:10).

Again we note that all apostles are disciples, but not all disciples are designated as apostles. Furthermore, other people beyond the twelve were named as apostles in Scripture. These included Barnabas and Paul (Acts 14:14 and Rom. 1:1); Silvanus and Timothy (1 Thess. 1:1–6); and Apollos (1 Cor. 4:6–9). Andronicus and Junias (named Junia in the earliest manuscripts, which would be a woman) were called apostles in Romans 16:7.

The Eastern church also names the seventy-two (some manuscripts say seventy) who were sent out by Jesus two by two "the Seventy Apostles." This scenario in Luke 10:1–24 entailed orders from Jesus to go out and heal the sick. Miracles were performed and demons were cast out.

Many believe that when those who saw Jesus personally (which historically includes Paul because of his face-to-face conversion with the Lord) passed away, there was to be a succession of apostles, passed down officially throughout the ages. This is not generally a Protestant tradition.

Some think that after those died who had seen Jesus, the apostolic office ceased altogether. Some believe it continues. Still others think that the office doesn't continue, but the apostolic work does. Again, I'm not here to quibble, and I at least believe that the apostolic work must and does continue. We've clearly seen that there's a sending current that flows from the heart and personality of God. We've also noted that this current is a major purpose for the church in the world. We've observed that God gives orders and sends people out, and we know that vital apostolic movements have occurred since the church began. These have changed the course of history.

God is the same yesterday, today, and tomorrow. In every biblical language He has provided for this concept of the emissary who is sent: in Hebrew, the *shaliach*, in Greek the apostle, and in Latin the missionary. God has called out those He has chosen to oversee this movement, and they are to go. This going, however, isn't just the job of a few "professional" missionaries. The whole church is to participate. Those who oversee the sending current engage the church with sending in its various forms. The overseers ensure the current's health and assure that participation in the current is integrated into the life and purpose of the local church. Without it, to put it bluntly, the church can't be what it is supposed to be.

PAUL, "THE BUNGLER"

I always viewed Paul as a mighty apostle—a strategist, a strong church planter who went around and planted church after church. This is undoubtedly a correct concept, but my mind shifted some when I was blessed by a free trip to Greece called "In the Footsteps of St. Paul." My husband and I had the wonderful opportunity to see Athens, Corinth, Berea, Ephesus, and Philippi, and in the process, Paul became real to me.

We were sitting by the river where Lydia, the dyer of purple cloth, was so affected by Paul. Let me put her story into context (Acts 16:6–12). Paul had wanted to go into Asia and preach. This was a good apostolic thought, but it wasn't from God. First of all, Paul had been traveling throughout Phrygia and Galatia "having been kept by the Holy Spirit from preaching the word in the province of Asia" (v. 6). Hmm . . . I wonder why?

Then Paul tried to enter Bithynia, "but the Spirit of Jesus would not allow them to" (v. 7). So they passed by and went down to Troas. There Paul had a vision "of a man of Macedonia standing and begging him, 'Come over to Macedonia and help us'" (v. 9).

Paul set out immediately, and by a series of stops and routes, he went to Philippi, which is "a Roman colony and the leading city of that district of Macedonia" (v. 12). Now the story with Lydia starts in verse 13. It was the Sabbath, and Paul and his companions went outside the city where they "expected to find a place of prayer." This is because it takes ten men to constitute a Jewish temple and if there weren't enough for one, the Jews in the area knew to gather by the river (notice that they were thinking of prayer and worship, not church planting.)

> *It means we don't need to have everything figured out, planned to the hilt, and perfectly designed.*

Only women were gathered by that river, so Paul began to speak (not preach, but speak) with the women who possibly had likewise gathered for prayer. One of those listening was Lydia. She was from Thyatira, a town in the territory of Lydia (whence she got her name), which specialized in cloth made of purple dye. She was also a "God-fearer," a term given by the Jews for someone who believed in God but had not yet become a full Jewish proselyte. "The Lord opened her heart to respond to Paul's message" (v. 14), and then she and her household were baptized.

Now come with me to the present day where I'm sitting by that same river. Our Greek guide explains that the purple dye comes from a shellfish (rather like a mollusk) that is available in only a few areas of the world. People would dive for the mollusks, and each one was so small that it gave only one drop of the purple dye.

Our guide said tradition has it that Lydia was in charge of the whole operation in that area for this particular trade union dealing in purple cloth. Think of the numbers of divers needed, the work of getting enough dye out of the shellfish to color something, and the connections required with those who wove the cloth and the designers for the garments. Then there was a need for sewing and shipping to places like Rome.

My Latin studies kicked in as I recalled that the Roman emperors wore purple clothing and the Roman senators were allowed to wear togas with a purple stripe. This was a special symbol of their wealth and power. No wonder. Think of the cost of these special clothes! It took 10,000 mollusks to dye one toga. The dye was rare, and the clothing was worth more than its weight in gold. Lydia was a wealthy woman.

Our Greek guide continued to say that when she invited Paul to come to her house, she would automatically have incorporated him into her wide network of connections. Her house was her office. This wide network helped to establish the foundation of a church. At that information from the guide, I rather had a mind warp. I had always viewed Paul as going in with plans and strategies and using his great intelligence to start churches wherever he went, but I believe I placed too much emphasis upon human skill.

Suddenly, my view of him switched a bit, and I coined the term "Paul, the Bungler." I mean no disrespect whatsoever. Paul just became a real man to me, and I loved his apostleship all the more for it. He wasn't overwhelmed with the work of planting a church. He was just living life and centering on God. Paul wandered down to the river to pray and to see if he could find any other Jews around. He kind of "bungled" his way—not at all aware of what God was about to do—found a group of women, spoke with them, and voila! God produced the necessary strategy to provide Paul with an instant church base of numerous connections and a place to meet. Lydia's wealth certainly couldn't hurt with resourcing either.

This insight into Paul's ministry is a relief. It means we don't need to have everything figured out, planned to the hilt, and perfectly designed. I'm not negating the value of those things; I'm saying there's a clear bottom line—*God will grow His church.*

The Lord had plans. He nudged Paul out of Asia, took him away from Bithynia, and sent him finally into Macedonia. There Paul ran into Lydia who was actually from Asia where he had wanted to go in the first place. But she was in Philippi, and she became the first documented European convert. God was already at work in Lydia's heart and she responded openly, with a church being established. The Philippian church was a blessing to Paul. His letter to it is warm, and he apparently had few problems with it.

God has plans, and one of the greatest things we can do is to discover what He is up to. Wherever He is already working, the effort will be so much easier, and God Himself will raise it up. Our task is to pray and stay close to Him, letting Him guide us each step of the way instead of running out with our own headstrong plans. We need to catch the wind of the Spirit and let Him take us where He wants us to go.

God knows where people's hearts are open. He wants to send us to people groups, to individuals, to particular age groups and cultural groups. He cares about the youth cults like the Goth subculture, still alive in Western Europe. Remember the great work among the beach and surfing crowds on the west coast in the 1960s through the Jesus People ministry? He can go anywhere and to anyone. What we must do is to listen to Him and go.

APOSTOLIC FUNCTIONS

First, we know that the main function of the apostolic overseers is that they are emissaries sent by God to certain places and people to accomplish His bidding. They're apt to be led into places where Satan has previously held reign and where the Enemy's darkness is presently prevailing. The apostolic task is to push back that darkness, pray through, intercede for those people, and do any necessary spiritual warfare until there's a breakthrough and people start getting saved.

Secondly, in order to accomplish all this we know that God provides miraculous signs so unbelievers can see for themselves that He is the only true One to serve. The apostolic work is to show, not just tell. The third mark of the apostolic work is God's power, grace, and love in all that is done. Signs are an important point, not a negotiable point, for anyone working in the apostolic. Signs and wonders accompanied all whom Jesus sent out, and they should still accompany those sent out today. If anyone has an apostolic calling, missing the miraculous doesn't mean they aren't called; it means they have some more praying to do regarding this matter.

Peter, in his famous message on the day of Pentecost, noted this: "Jesus of Nazareth was a man accredited by God to you by miracles, wonders, and signs, which God did among you through him, as you yourselves know" (Acts 2:22).

Having been involved in the accreditation processes for colleges and universities in the Midwest, I know firsthand that it isn't a simple and easy process to get accredited. There must be documentation and proof for everything, and all parts of university life are studied carefully. With this personal backdrop in place, I realize Peter was saying a great deal when he noted that Jesus was accredited by God. What a stamp of approval! His documentation was the miracles, wonders, and signs, but it was also his life. Paul even refers to his own documentation as a true apostle when he states, "I persevered in demonstrating among you the marks of a true apostle, including signs, wonders and miracles" (2 Cor. 12:12).

A third mark of an apostle isn't an easy one. In 2 Corinthians 11:16–33 and 12:1–13, Paul lists some of his sufferings, persecutions, insults, weaknesses, church burdens, and pressures. This is also how we can tell true apostolic emissaries. They're willing to serve and are likely to pay a great price to serve in this role. Since they're pushing back the darkness, there will be satanic backlash.

The New Testament apostles were flogged numerous times, pulled before the Sanhedrin for questioning, and thrown into prison. Those prisons weren't nice buildings with cells but were rude holes in the ground—dark, damp, and barred.

Mobs got angry and tried to kill the apostles time and time again. The apostles were insulted, pushed around, shipwrecked, slandered, doubted, and afflicted. Going into the dark places to do the work of God isn't for the faint-hearted or for those who aren't called.

In Acts 20:24 Paul stated, "However, I consider my life worth nothing to me; my only aim is to finish the race and complete the task the Lord Jesus has given me—the task of testifying to the good news of God's grace." Anyone who moves out as an apostolic emissary has to have this matter decided in this way.

In the midst of these challenges, the New Testament apostles were characterized by boldness. Often they even prayed for more of it, which usually meant they would get into still more trouble, but they were willing to share the gospel regardless of the consequences.

Fourth, the apostles moved around among different cultural situations. They were adept at contextualizing the gospel. The church wasn't established in an old Jewish form but in new and innovative ways that fit each culture. The church leadership was local and indigenous; the church was self-governing, self-sustaining, and self-propagating. Each church had the opportunity to translate the truth into their context.

Fifth, the apostles also played the role of connecting the churches and networking people. Since they were traveling around, they often carried letters from place to place, brought news of how the various works were doing, and led people into prayer for other churches and territories. They were also resource developers, taking up offerings to help with needs in different cities.

Sixth, it should be noted that Paul often talked about his laboring so he wouldn't be a burden upon anybody. As a tentmaker, Paul seemed to be active at this work, as well as being an apostolic church planter. He wasn't out money-grubbing. This meant he made other connections in society. It also allowed him to move easily from place to place—to pick up and go when the Spirit prompted.

Seventh, the apostles strove to maintain proper doctrine in all of the churches they planted. Paul's letters are full of this doctrinal guidance—sometimes reemphasizing certain truths, other times correcting. This is an important part of the sending current.

Forging out correct doctrine and guarding the gospel's important points are a significant part of this flow. We need people who will be careful to prevent any digression from truth within the church.

Finally, in the places where churches were established, there was the necessity of dealing with their various troubles. A part of the apostolic work is to keep the churches healthy in every way. The apostles would begin a church and move on, but they still kept contact with all the churches they had started. They handled controversies, people problems, schisms, disputes, irregularities, and other difficulties. We see Paul's letters working to assist in these various areas.

God uses apostolic workers to be an independent and unbiased help in times of church conflict. They can assist in properly taking care of pastors who have fallen or need assistance with strengthening or rehabilitation. These overseers are certainly gifts to the church.

Paul noted, "Besides everything else, I face daily the pressure of my concerns for all the churches" (2 Cor. 11:28). Truly, the calling is a weight, but people who are anointed as apostolic emissaries are prepared by God to handle it. He gives them wisdom, strength, courage, and insight. God Himself leads them

It's apparent that the New Testament apostles were generally respected by the churches they founded, since the local church teams went back to them for advice. This is as it should be. The previous apostolic work should be honored by those who are now building upon it. After all, the apostles and the prophets are the ones who laid the foundation for that church according to Ephesians 2:20.

This setup is necessary because the apostles are called to move on to another work, but they still care about what they're leaving behind. Those with an apostolic calling won't be able to stick around one place or with one work for long. By the nature and calling of the apostolic emissary, God will send them to a new thing. They'll get restless and know that it's time to move on and establish something new.

APOSTOLIC WORK TODAY

Apostolic work includes—but isn't limited to—foreign missionaries, home missionaries, church planters, and often superintendents of regions and designated groups. Let's briefly consider each one.

Foreign missionaries are generally considered to be apostolic. This is a reasonable conclusion since they're sent out by God and the church to foreign lands in order to establish the church. I believe the majority of missionaries have an apostolic anointing for their work. Home missionaries are also usually apostolic. They often go to special people groups who need attention, and God has sent them to make inroads. Home missionaries work with the deaf, with people at rodeos and racetracks, with the disabled, with prisoners, and in many other capacities.

When I said these are "generally apostolic," I've noted some exceptions. Some foreign missionaries are primarily educators, working in the foreign Bible schools or in other teaching venues. Sometimes missionaries are primarily pastoral, their main function being to pastor a church overseas. Some are evangelists, and prophetic voices. All of this is possible for home missionaries with some being pastors, some teaching, and so forth.

A chief task of missionaries is to prime the apostolic flow in their sending churches by sharing about their mission field and by hosting mission teams, thus helping move people outside their church walls. Missionaries also share the apostolic sending flow with their foreign church. As the new churches grow, mature, and become strong, the Lord would have those believers go out as well.

Once I was in another country at a conference when I felt I had a word from God for them regarding this. I wasn't the one who was scheduled to speak, but before I knew it, someone told me they felt I had the word, and I was on the platform with a long time slot turned over to me. I was totally surprised since I hadn't said anything to anybody, but the Lord was clearly orchestrating something.

I preached what was on my heart. At that time this nation had sent few missionaries overseas, and the prevailing tendency was to support any they did send for only a year or so and then leave them to their own devices. Most had to return home. God wanted His apostolic sending current to flow more strongly from this country. The crux of the message the Lord had given me was that either they got more concerned with supporting missionaries and praying earnestly for other lands or the Lord would remove the blessings He had been sending them. It was a strong message, and afterwards I knelt down on the stage to pray, the presence of the Lord overpowering me.

What happened was that in the next four hours, I could not move; I really could not. The group was supposed to have the afternoon free, but they didn't eat lunch or go anywhere. Instead, they prayed for hours, one after another leading at the microphone for the nations and cities of the world, repenting and crying out to God. When I could get up finally, not a single person had left the auditorium, as far as I could tell. Every seat was still filled, and people were praying everywhere.

It is my joy to report that through the service and organizational help of some missionaries in that place, they exponentially expanded their missions sending all over the world. Sending is

God's heart, not just from the United States but from churches all over the world. It is to their benefit to have this flow, as it is to ours.

Church planters should also be apostolic. They are laying a foundation where there has been inadequate church presence before. Perhaps some church plants fail because the planters weren't prepared for the battle that Satan would wage. Also, we've seen the importance of doing things God's way as He did with Lydia. Our plans may not be His plans; it's vital that we listen to His directions.

God wants the new churches to become apostolic in their turn. Church planters shouldn't simply be planting a local congregation that takes care of itself but one that reaches out and does apostolic work in its community and abroad. If this design is part of the founding vision of a new church, it will think and work in fresh ways to move out beyond itself.

Another role that is most often apostolic is that of district superintendent or state overseer. Consider their tasks of being aware of their territory, of knowing where churches should be planted and where the darkness needs to be pushed back. They lead their people to pray for these things and to mobilize resources.

Their oversight of the churches includes resolving conflict, keeping the DNA of doctrinal correctness, dealing with error, handling leadership failure and issues, providing wisdom and perspective, networking churches, and keeping the churches and leadership healthy.

There are many other examples of the apostolic functioning all around us that we need to observe. Those who work with groups that interconnect various denominations within a city, a region, a state, a country, or among various nations are often apostolic. Those who have founded such movements as the following were sent by the Lord to meet a particular need and extend the kingdom of God: Youth for Christ, the Navigators, InterVarsity Christian Fellowship, Youth with a Mission (YWAM), the Fellowship of Christian Athletes, Promise Keepers, L'Abri Fellowship, Focus on the Family, Student Venture, the National Association of Evangelicals, Walk Thru the Bible, Mercy Ships, Young Life, Special Forces, Chi Alpha, World Relief, and Convoy of Hope. Unsion is Hispanic television with a Christian worldview housed in Ecuador but stretching from Canada to Argentina. It has seen nearly 7,000 decisions for Christ in one year on their counseling program alone.[40] We could note many other Christian groups, but suffice it to say that people involved in these types of ministries are often apostolic.

Wherever you see someone or a group going into a new area where they have noted a need and wish to meet it, you probably have apostolic work involved. Apostolic emissaries are frequently creative, rather on the edge, eager to try new things, willing to brave risk, and fearless.

Although apostolic overseers are often involved outside of the church, we can frequently find some of these same traits and callings within our local churches. God often provides us with apostolic types who will incite the local church to reach out into new territory. These people are regularly coming up with novel ideas and have a way of making the links and forging the connections necessary to make things happen.

Such people might be frustrating because sometimes they appear never to be satisfied. They aren't happy with the status quo and seem constantly to want change. When one project is completed, they like to leave it with another person to manage and move on to change something else.

The apostolic workers in the church include the change agent, the entrepreneur, the creative imaginary, the "what if" person, the mover-and-shaker, the risk-taker, the innovator, the networker, the gap-filler, the resourcing individual, the brave kingdom warrior, the denominational connector, the contextualizer, the miracle worker, the mobilizer, the cross-culturally astute, and one sensitive to special groups. If they're hearing from God, count them as a gift to the church instead of troublemakers.

This miraculous sending current is meant to flow around the world and within the church. It flows to communities, regions, states, and countries. There are no boundaries to its swooshing flow, and we need it desperately. Most of all we need it to take us out of ourselves, and when we let it flow, the results are stupendous.

As a local church, it's God's pleasure and plan that we participate in some mighty big thrusts. His strategies and ways are various and inclusive. For our own sakes, the local church needs to embrace this expanding and extending current sent from the heart of God.

THINGS TO CONSIDER . . .

1. God continues to send out people to do His work. Do you think the church is doing what it's supposed to do if it isn't moving out into the world at God's instructions? How much "sending" and "moving out" are happening in your church? Give examples.

2. The apostolic current moves into dark places held by Satan. To invade his camp means that this thrust must be accompanied by the power of the Holy Spirit and prayer. How are people in your church taking up this fight?

3. What does the study of "Paul the Bungler" teach us?

4. Name some of the hallmarks of a person who is moving in the apostolic.

5. Where do you observe the apostolic work of God right now?

Chapter Thirteen

WE SHALL NOT CEASE FROM EXPLORATION

⸻ ✧ ⸻

Seeing through the lens of the five gifts Jesus gave to the church focuses our thinking upon what is crucial for the church today. The five currents are what God sees as important for the church to function in a vital and healthy way. They come straight from His heart.

Those five gifts fill the roles that oversee these currents. They are vital because they watch over and guard the currents' drift, strength, and freedom from debris. Without them, each current won't receive the attention, nurture, care, and level of attention that it should. These roles aren't the main emphases, however. What is significant are the currents they superintend. To put it another way: why focus upon leadership if we don't care passionately about what they lead moving through the entire church?

We need to stretch our thinking past the "five-fold ministry" and emphasize the moving forth that God wants to see in His church. This flow involves not only the leadership but all those in the church who are ministering in these various currents. Remember in Ephesians 4 that the purpose of the leadership roles was to "train the people to do the work of the ministry." As all work together under the headship of God, the currents will pour forth in fresh and powerful ways. With the five currents in operation, all aspects of a revitalized church will surge and the church will be on the move. Here's what it will look like:

The Powerful Wooing Current: We'll constantly have people coming to Christ because the church is sharing, loving, reaching out, and wooing others to Him. Those working in this current have been empowered by God through the baptism in the Holy Spirit and His constant presence with them. They say exactly what He wants them to say in order to reach souls with the good news.

The Radical Forming Current: The new believers become disciples and followers of Jesus, learning to hear and obey His voice, growing and maturing to be more like Him. They produce the fruit of the Spirit and build a close relationship with each member of the Trinity. Those working in this current are strong spiritual models for those they are forming. They communicate and apply the Scriptures accurately and lead people in the spiritual disciplines.

The Synchronized Choreography Current: The church is healthy, being cared for, and guarded. People are functioning together well as a body of believers and using the gifts of the Spirit on a regular basis. They prefer one another in love, give space to others to be themselves, and take their place in the body of Christ to serve as God designs and instructs. Those working in this movement are no respecter of persons; they care for everyone. They know people by name, are aware of what is happening to them, minister to their needs, and go after them when they wander off.

The Housecleaning Directional Current: The church is secure and holy. God is directing it and correcting it as needed; it is receiving confirmation, exhortation, edification, and sometimes warning. The church gives God time to speak and reveal His plans in the midst of business and assembly. Those working in this movement are prayer warriors and intercessors. They function in both formal and informal ways and carry around a large toolbox for handling various prophetic situations. They're in tune with God, His heart, His tone, His timing, and His approach.

The Miraculous Sending Current: The sending movement is strong, with the church able to look outside of itself, take back territory that Satan has previously held, work in signs and wonders to establish God's might, build connections and networks, and maintain sound doctrine and purity within the body of Christ. Those who work in this current are anointed as God's representatives; He sends them to various countries, cultural groups, and problem areas. They are innovators, entrepreneurs, church extenders and planters, risk-takers, and guardians of the core truths of the church. They consistently move on to take new territory or tasks.

THE OVERSEERS

Those whom Jesus gave as gifts must motivate people in the church to be a part of the currents. They are to identify believers with the skill set, heart cry, personality, natural gifting, interest, and anointing from God to participate. Overseers should always be searching for those who have the flow of the current already springing up in their inner being. Then, according to Ephesians 4, the overseers are to train these people to do the work of the service. The overseers will engage and encourage them, prepare and support them.

All five overseers are not doing their assigned work of equipping others in the church today. This is a prime undertaking, and we dare not abandon it. The overseers must purposely find ways to train others to participate effectively in their current. They should identify young people who may have a call and allow them to walk alongside in various ministry contexts.

These efforts of the overseers bring important results according to Ephesians. It builds up the body and develops unity in the faith and in the knowledge of the Son of God. The church—the bride—will "become mature, attaining to the whole measure of the fullness of Christ" (Eph. 4:13).

God has provided the means to bring the church to maturity. We dare not eschew it, especially in these end days. The Ephesians verses in chapter 4 that were provided as a backdrop for this book contain a last section that we haven't yet considered:

> Then we will no longer be infants, tossed back and forth by the waves, and blown here and there by every wind of teaching and by the cunning and craftiness of people in their deceitful scheming. Instead, speaking the truth in love, we will grow to become in every respect the mature body of him who is the head, that is, Christ. From him the whole body, joined and held together by every supporting ligament, grows and builds itself up in love, as each part does its work. (Eph. 4:14–16)

In these last days before Jesus returns, the Lord prophesied that the times would be rough. He warned that false messiahs and prophets would appear who would deceive, if they could, even the elect (Mark 13:22). When all the currents are working as they should, the church will no longer act like children who are tossed about and easily swayed.

The health of the church is at stake. The preparation of the bride for the coming of the Bridegroom is the question at hand. Whether everyone who is supposed to will make it into heaven is at issue.

The parable of the ten virgins in Matthew 25:1–7 shows us the necessity of getting prepared for our Lord's return and having the oil of the Holy Spirit in full measure. In this parable, it appears that when Jesus, the Bridegroom, comes back for His bride, some

> *If we abandon or ignore one of the currents, we neglect a significant characteristic and work of God Himself; we don't have a complete picture of who He is.*

won't be ready. In fact, as many as half the church may not be ready. This is most serious business.

I believe the overseers of the currents must see that people are warned and prepared. They need to be brought to God, where the Holy Spirit will provide them with the oil needed to keep their torches burning until Jesus returns for His bride. Taking time with God and being in His presence is how we collect oil and have enough to take us through.

It's also the only way that all of the currents can flow. Remember that the members of the Trinity are the ones who originate, instigate, generate, activate, disseminate, circulate, and perpetuate the flow. There is no flow without God.

The overseers must lead people to Him first and foremost. Otherwise we aren't moving anywhere and, worse yet, we won't be ready for His return. No oil. No light. No entry to the wedding feast of the Lamb.

A REVELATION OF GOD

We all need a fuller revelation of who God is and how He wants to work. All of these currents that issue forth from Him help with this great task. They show us what is on His heart and emphasize those aspects He most values. If we abandon or ignore one of the currents, we neglect a significant characteristic and work of

God Himself; we don't have a complete picture of who He is. A more comprehensive understanding enhances our worship.

Worship entails more than singing some songs. Worship is truly worship when we're drawn into the presence of Almighty God and our vision of how big He is takes hold of us. Worship can and should happen through the flow of every single current. We realize what He has done for us in every area and our souls rejoice in praise to Him! This is much more meaningful in content than some of the songs that seem to focus more on ourselves than on God.

Different attributes of who God is reveal themselves in each current. Jesus as the teacher, prophet, shepherd, evangelist, and apostle show us varying facets of His work and personality. He shimmers and shines as a gem when the light bounces off His various workings. This is true of Jesus, the Father, and the Holy Spirit, all three.

Every single member of the Trinity is intimately and integrally involved in every one of the currents. We've already established their work and initiation so that the flows will be strong. The currents aren't acts of people, though God chooses to use us. They are accomplished by God Himself. Only in Him can the currents flow freely. All five currents originate in Him, and He propels and energizes each one. He directs, guides, and safeguards them. He is the prime mover.

THE NEED FOR GOD

We aren't much without God. I sometimes think of myself like a violin. I will do all I can to become the best instrument possible, and this includes education, commitment, hard work, faithfulness, reading and continued learning, openness to correction, the spiritual disciplines, and growing in any way I can. Still, with all this, I know that even the best Stradivarius violin is nothing until it is played by a master violinist.

We're desperate for Jesus. Remember John 15:5: "I am the vine; you are the branches. If you remain in me and I in you, you will bear much fruit; apart from me you can do nothing." Nothing will count without Him. The hard work and effort will come to nothing without Him. Everything will collapse without Him. Jesus is the center.

In Exodus 33:15–16, Moses poignantly begged God, "If your Presence does not go with us, do not send us up from here. How will anyone know that you are pleased with me and with your people unless you go with us? What else will distinguish me and your people from all the other people on the face of the earth?"

Perhaps our greatest problem in the church today is that we've gotten comfortable without His presence. We hope He comes, but if He doesn't, we're willing to attempt it all on our own. In fact, we've gotten so comfortable without His presence that even when He does show up, we may not want to stop and turn over the reins.

We've become secure in our own control, though I'm not sure why we feel so safe. After all, are we really in charge? What can we keep from happening? Is what we want so perfect after all?

Oars may give us a sense of directing our own lives, but what difference will they make when the storm comes up? Our controlling is a flimsy excuse for having our own way and following God only when we feel like it. These are some tough words, but the admonition is directed at the crux of our present church problems.

We bemoan what is happening over and over again, but we don't go to God for the answers. We attend conferences and look for ideas that will work, when He has a particular and perfect plan. We place people up on stage and put on a fine-tuned performance, when folks in the pews simply want to see the Father, to view the Son high and lifted up, to sense the power of the Spirit. We have to get back to saying, like Moses, "Unless you go with us, God, do not send us up."

Indeed, Moses correctly asked what would distinguish them from all the other people on the face of the earth if God did not go with them. The point is: Nothing. Nothing distinguishes us—only Him. He makes the difference. He is the answer.

We think that becoming relevant to society will draw people in. When they get there, however, they don't need more of the same. They need God, pure and simple. They need to know that *He* can make a difference. People have to recognize the Lord as the distinguishing factor.

If God isn't present, the only distinguishing factor is how well we're doing in contrast to someplace or somebody else. If another church or a coffee shop or a favorite chair is better, folks will go there. The presence of God, however . . . now that can change everything!

If we want to keep step with the Spirit, He must lead us (Gal. 5:25). We have to sense His desires, His nudges and movements, and then we must follow. When two try to lead, we have a disaster, and that's a pretty fair picture of much of the church in the United States today. God wants to lead His church. He has plans for it right now, but we have to do it His way and not ours. This will happen only as we relinquish, pray, spend time with Him, listen to what He has to say, and obey His directions. We must connect to the Vine and stay attached constantly.

Once I had a vivid dream. I could see various musicians getting ready for a big concert. It was time to start, but things weren't right. Some of the musicians weren't in their seats. Some were in their seats but didn't have their instruments with them. Others had not taken their instruments out of their cases. A few had their instruments out, but weren't tuned up or at the ready, attentive position. Pages of music were in various stages of disarray.

The curtains opened, but few of the musicians were prepared. The orchestra leader stepped up and tapped his baton on the stand, calling everyone to respond for the beginning of the piece. As they all tried to catch up, the disarray was more than obvious. The director raised his arms to conduct the piece, but many musicians were still messing with their instruments or trying to find the page they were supposed to be on. Of course, the music they produced sounded horrible; nobody was in the same place and most weren't playing.

I woke up and my spirit sank. I knew it was a picture of the church. I believe that God wants to bring a great, last-days revival that will sweep thousands into the kingdom. But we aren't ready for it. We aren't paying attention to the conductor. And we had better change that, pronto!

INTO THE CURRENTS WITHOUT AN OAR

What will you decide to do? Will you listen to God and obey? Will you spend time with Him and hear what He has to say about His plans instead of asking Him to bless yours? Will you stop trying to find the answers to the problems in the church in all the wrong places? Will you turn over the reins and do it God's way?

What is your choice? Stay on shore and play it safe? Or get into the coracle and go for a ride on the currents? What will you opt for? Stay inside your walls where the wind can't get to you? Or let the wind of the Spirit propel you to unknown territory?

Are you frightened? Will you revert to what you know and to whatever seems safe? Or will you trust Him? Will you decide that maintaining the illusion of control will be a better lifestyle for you? Or will you take off without a rudder or an oar?

Will you stay with your own well-designed plans and comforts? Or will you lay down your life to go where He wishes to take you? Do you have to know the end before you even set out?

Or will you go without knowing anything more than that He is totally reliable and you will follow Him to the ends of the earth no matter what comes?

Is God's mission more important to you than staying in your comfy place? Do you really care about lost souls? Will you risk absolutely everything so that others might be saved? I mean *everything*: reputation, the possibility of deprivation, the loss of personal ease and satisfaction?

Will you do it God's way instead of yours? His methods are often edgy and unusual; is that all right with you? Will you let the Holy Spirit be like the wild goose or will you squeeze Him into a dovecote and clamp down the door?

You're going to put down this book in a moment. The coracle is leaving. Are you going to hop in or not? If you close the cover without jumping in, you'll be left on the shore. We're off . . . the church on the move to catch the wind of the Spirit!

A postscript: Are you in the boat? Good.

Just remember that unless the currents are flowing, we'll be dead in the water. Not fun in the middle of the ocean. If we have only one current flowing, we may well be going around in circles. If almost all of them are flowing, but one or two are missing or neglected, we're likely to get off-target and not come out where God intended.

Then there is the wind of the Holy Spirit. If we don't let Him blow into our hoisted sails, we won't move very well. The Holy Spirit helps us on our way. He is the Paraclete, the One called alongside to help. How we need His help! Blow us, Holy Spirit. Move us on, Lord!

Let's keep exploring, because there's so much more to see and do. The Holy Spirit and the currents of God will take us for a ride, and what an adventure it will be as we catch the wind of the Spirit!

THINGS TO CONSIDER . . .

1. The five currents are summarized in this chapter. Which currents do you think are strongest in your church? Which are the weakest? Which have strong leadership oversight and which do not? Evaluate the state of affairs for your church.

2. Now think about these currents in the church of God as a whole today. Which currents do you think are flowing the most strongly and which are flowing the weakest?

3. What can be done in your church to increase the flow of the weakest currents?

4. Discuss the importance of having the presence of God individually and as a church. What about this? How much is this a prime desire for you? What can be done to connect even better with God and keep Him central?

5. Throughout history there have been strong moves of God that have changed history. We need Him to do it again! What can we learn from them?

6. What did you decide? Will you get into the coracle or not? How do you anticipate your life may be different, depending upon your decision?

Chapter Fourteen

LET'S CHAT

✧

Often when I teach or preach on the five ministry gifts, there are a lot of questions. They are important to consider, and I wanted to include some of them here along with a few thoughts. I trust this will help us sort through some of the implications and application of what we've been considering. I also hope you'll feel like you're across a table from me, and we're chatting back and forth over a good cup of Java.

1. Is everybody in the church involved in one of these five gifts as an overseer?

No, this isn't what Scripture tells us at all. Remember, only "some" were given in each of these roles according to Ephesians 4. Also recall that their main task was to train people to do the work of the ministry. This means that most church members won't be in one of these five overseer roles, although they may have personal interests, personalities, and skill sets that make them particularly interested in a certain area. After they're trained to do the work of the ministry in their area(s) of service, they'll likely jump in to help in those places and God will use them in wonderful ways.

2. I see people who seem to be in several of these five roles. Is that possible?

Oh, yes. People sometimes start in one role and God moves them into another. For example, an individual may begin in a pastoral role and then be taken into an apostolic role. That's just one example and there are many possible shifts God could carry forth. He's the One who makes the determinations.

Also, I believe that people can have a strong role that is their primary gift to the church, but then there can be one or even two back-up roles. Pastor and teacher often go together, for example. Paul mentions several roles for himself in 2 Timothy 1:11, and Peter was both an apostle and an evangelist to the Gentiles. Remember, though, that no one has all the roles.

3. How do I know which role I am in or if I even am in one?

Sometimes a person who is already in a particular role will recognize it in you and talk with you about it. By a prophetic word this is also sometimes the case. Note that throughout Scripture the prophets often understood a calling through the Spirit and anointed others (e.g., Samuel anointing Saul as king and calling out David from among his brothers).

Even with all of this, however, it's most important that you hear from God about the matter. He is the One who calls, anoints, and gives these gifts to the church. No one can decide the calling for himself or herself, and you shouldn't accept anybody else's assessment if you have no inner witness to its veracity. Let the Lord speak to you.

4. Could it be that I have been called to one of these five roles and don't know it?

Yes. I believe that our lack of understanding about these roles has left many people without an awareness of their role. It's like having the mantle placed over your shoulders by God but you don't realize it's there and you don't act upon it.

This can be a serious problem. If God wants to use you in a certain capacity but you don't know it, that weakens your functioning in it with the strength and confidence God desires. The Lord wants you to realize the anointing and all the resources He has placed upon your life so you can act against Satan with the authority God intends. Know the mantle that is upon you and stand up tall into it.

5. Do things look differently after I step up to the plate?

Most assuredly! When you know your calling, it's like receiving a new lens from God. He will help you to see things through that lens. When you have to determine where God might be calling you to next, for example, He helps you regard the choices based upon considerations such as how much the gifting will be used. He quite often makes "promotions" that look to others like you're going lower (in title, position, or salary) whereas, in reality, He's expanding your ability to serve in His kingdom work.

God will assist you in seeing these things according to His viewpoint. Even looking through your everyday tasks with your God-given lens will help you to make choices and decisions, set priorities, face your problems with a new insight, and stay strong in the midst of the battle.

6. How do I get training for my role?

The first place to go is to God's Word. Study everything there is in Scripture about your calling. Consider good examples and what they did and said. Ponder their attitudes, their faithfulness, and what they endured. The Spirit is the best teacher, and He will show you.

After that, study any negative words or persons: the false side. Ask the Lord to show you what to avoid, and pray never to fall into these wrong perspectives.

As the Lord leads, try walking out what He calls you to do in your role. Remember that you are learning, and give yourself the chance to grow and even fail. Be willing to practice in an environment of grace. You will learn from your mistakes. As you go back to the Lord, He'll forgive you, assure your heart, and continue the training process.

If you know of a more mature person who is functioning in the role to which you feel called, watch them. Don't be afraid to ask them questions and spend time with them whenever you can like Joshua did with Moses. See if that person is willing to mentor you.

Remember that your best teacher is God Himself. Do what Joshua did. Stay longer than your mentor in the presence on the Lord.

7. On the flip slide, how do we best encourage others, particularly young people, who are trying to determine if they are in one of the five roles?

We should keep our eyes open for young people who seem committed to the Lord and appear to have some of those traits needed to function within a particular role.

Let us say you are a pastor and you note a young person who cares for others, listens to them, seems to be burdened when one isn't doing well, and goes after someone who is straying from God. Talk with them, listen to their heart, answer their questions, and perhaps be a mentor. You can invite the young person to tag along when you do ministry work like visitation and give them opportunities to participate in various aspects of ministry.

This approach can happen for each of the roles, even the prophetic. I've enjoyed hosting "labs" where the spiritual gifts are in operation. They are informal times of waiting on God with others who are "safe." The ground rules are that anyone who feels like they have a word or any of the gifts of the Spirit should share it. If it is wrong, this is a learning time; we will talk about it and it will be okay. Often God gives identical words and encourages believers through confirmation to step out in faith.

You can also encourage young people as they discover what God is saying to them about their place in the church . . . either as one of the five gifts to the church or as a church member who participates in a current. Help them explore in safety and provide opportunities to try out some things and learn if it is for them. Listen to them with your heart and be faithful to affirm and gently correct as needed. So many are looking for this help and guidance!

8. I think I know what role I have, but nobody else does. What do I do?

If you know your role, pray, and God will open doors. See places that match the gifting and need your service; then offer to help. Watch your attitude; be humble; wait on the Lord, and then walk through any opening He provides. Trust in Him.

9. Nobody gives me a title or treats me with respect.

So what? Next question please.

Okay, I know that was a little tacky, but I couldn't resist. Seriously, if you think about it, you'll realize that not everybody recognized Jesus or His title and role as the Messiah. Many showed Him heaps of disrespect. We aren't above our Master. Now that's the real answer. We do well to stop focusing upon and feeling sorry for ourselves. Jesus is the center, not us, and we'll get our reward in due time if we remain faithful. We are called to endure suffering and pick up our cross every day and follow Him.

10. I know people who have the title of pastor but are in another role. What about that? Aren't there other mix-ups in the roles also?

Oh, yes, this is a problem with many facets. First of all, sometimes congregations have hired a pastor who is really a teacher. He doesn't relate so well with the people, and they get upset when he doesn't make hospital calls or care so much about the individuals. But they hired an anointed teacher, not a pastor, so what can they expect?

Likewise, sometimes churches will have special services with a traveling evangelist. However, no one gets saved at all throughout the meetings. The teaching was sure good though! Oh, I see, we brought in a traveling teacher.

Or we put someone on the mission field, but he wants to pastor a church there. Yes, we probably have a pastor and not an apostolic type.

Sometimes we have apostles trying to pastor a church. They get new works started and travel a lot, and that's great. However the people are left without a pastor to care for them and while the apostle is gone, the church can become most unhealthy and hurt.

These are just a few examples, but the roles are quite often confused today, both by the church and by the people called to those roles.

11. What happens when the five roles get mixed up like that?

If we don't recognize the calling and gifting of God upon people, we'll place them in the wrong spots and expect things out of them that they can't possibly deliver. They haven't been anointed for that and, important as it is, they won't come through. If they can't perform what they think they should, that makes them feel inadequate, unhappy, and unfulfilled. The expectations of the church won't be met, and the parishioners will be upset. In the midst of all this, however, we have simply mistitled and misappropriated the gifting. Put these well-meaning people called by God into the right spot and all will be well.

12. Why do we name almost all leadership roles in the church as pastor of this or that?

I don't know. We seem to be weighted toward pastors, don't we? However, we often have people in other roles who are being called pastor; for example, that administrative pastor, might that person actually be a prophetic voice? Or perhaps that music pastor is a prophetic person. Or the small groups pastor is an evangelist. Or the person starting new ministries all of the time is really in the apostolic role. Start looking around, and God will make it evident where His true gifts are lodged. Furthermore, why call a teacher a teaching pastor . . . unless, of course, there is a dual calling. Things would be much clearer if we named people accurately and just did some training on the nomenclature.

13. Having a clear team seems like it would be helpful.

Yes, having people who are sensitive to the five currents will keep the church's decision-making more balanced and the ministry currents flowing like they should. Each current needs people who are involved in it and advocating for it. Instead of getting upset with people who are always harping on a particular current, we ought to be thankful for them. Likewise, it's easy to get irritated with people who don't see things as we do when, in reality, we ought to be glad. We need the different viewpoints in order to have a fully moving church.

The various influences for the five currents may come from many sources within the church, but they might especially arise from outside connections, deacons and elders, and church staff. Thankfully, a team approach is approved by society in general, so this should be appealing right now. Not everything has to weigh upon the pastor. There's a set of checks and balances with this God-given approach as well.

14. Do each of the five gifts have a corresponding false side?

Yes, indeed they do. False prophets are mentioned in numerous places throughout Scripture, often with strict forewarnings. False teachers are mentioned in 1 Timothy 1:3–7 and 2 Peter 2:1–3, and we are cautioned against their destructive heresies, false doctrine, and exploitation. The church at Ephesus was commended in Revelation 2:2 for testing those who called themselves apostles but were not. Paul also warns against those who "are false apostles, deceitful workers, masquerading as apostles of Christ" in 2 Corinthians 11:13. Watch for the masks!

False shepherds (pastors) are discussed in Ezekiel 34. The Lord says to watch out for those who only take care of themselves instead of the flock. These false shepherds live well off the flock, but they "have not strengthened the weak or healed the sick or bound up the injured." They also have not gone out after the strays nor searched for the lost. They rule harshly, and the flock is scattered because there is no shepherd, ultimately being plundered and becoming food for the wild animals. Obviously

God doesn't like this state of affairs and says He's against these shepherds and will hold them accountable.

The term *false evangelist* is not directly provided in Scripture. There are speakers, however, who have engaging personalities and can provide outgoing and funny personas from the pulpit, but they preach false doctrine and a false God. People can be converted to a false God instead of to the one, true God. Timothy was charged to do the work of an evangelist (2 Tim. 4:5), and Paul warned him about providing careful instruction. Paul said, "For the time will come when people will not put up with sound doctrine" (2 Tim. 4:3).

For every one of the five gifts, it is possible to have a negative, deceitful, false, or incorrect side.

15. Why do these false sides occur?

Satan doesn't bother with anything that doesn't matter. If these roles each operated the way it should and all the corresponding currents were robust, the church would be so strong that the Devil would never win the battle against it or be able to take it down. Of course, we know he won't win in the end, but he's sure going to try. If he can knock out the acceptance of any of these five gifts from Jesus, he has gained tremendous ground. If he can weaken them in any way, he will attempt to do so.

Remember that Jesus saw these as the most precious gifts of His victory over Satan. So Satan realizes they're important, and he's going to go after them. He fabricates them, putting false and deceitful people into the roles and hopes that folks either won't notice or will get so frustrated that they'll write it all off. Satan slips in his demonic and human emissaries who are prideful, power-mongering, and unruly. He tries to deceive, if he can, even the elect.

If he can cripple any of the overseer roles so that those called by the Lord can barely function, he has one gigantic win.

16. Are there still people in these false roles today?

Yes, definitely. I've heard of people who have named themselves as apostles, gone into regions, and told the pastors there that they are now the apostles over their churches. They wheedle their way in with slick talk and false perspectives. They insist upon oversight of those churches and demand 10 percent of the offerings. What? This is not of God!

Some self-proclaimed prophets have given "words" as from God but they were false words. The people were led astray. Likewise, some teachers and also pastors are sharing false doctrine and leading people away from the truth. The false twists and spins, the inappropriate emphases, as well as truth that is neglected and left out, all these lead people away from truth. Jesus prophesied this would happen in the last days.

17. What can we do to counteract these false roles?

We must stay close to God and remain in the Word—His Word is truth! We must pray for discernment and allow the Holy Spirit to lead us into all truth. If we don't, even we could go awry.

Just because there are false, satanic sides possible for each of the five treasures Jesus provided to the church, doesn't mean we should put the true gifts aside or minimize them. We must be able to recognize the deceitful imitations and spurn those, while we simultaneously note the true gifts from God and embrace them. For the false, watch for the masks, the lack of integrity, missing fruit of the Spirit, incorrect doctrine, and selfish ambition. For the true, appreciate the humility, the wholeness and integrity, sharing of the truth, a servant attitude, and caring for others, even at personal cost.

18. Who is the leader in the midst of all this?

God is the leader. He is the head and the only head. Colossians 1:18 states, "And he is the head of the body, the church; he is the beginning and the firstborn from among the dead, so that in everything he might have the supremacy." Jesus is the head of the church, and we must pay attention to Him. This is the way to be a united, well-functioning, and active body.

19. But aren't we all supposed to strive to be leaders? Leadership is important. Look at all the books on the subject!

If everybody is supposed to be a leader, who are the followers? Why is leadership considered the ideal? God's choices, His anointing, His gifting, His enabling, His empowering, His strength and His own resources . . . this is God's way, not a perfectly developed set of leadership skills.

We worry far too much about who is the human leader. Any movement that seeks to make everybody a leader is off-kilter. If anything, it's exactly the opposite. Jesus said, "Whoever serves me must follow me, and where I am, my servant also will be" (John 12:26). We aren't all aspiring leaders. We're all inspired followers!

If anything, the people in these five roles are under everybody else, serving them, washing their feet, laying down their very lives for them. They don't lord it over others but instead encourage others to rise up even higher—to stand on their shoulders, if you will.

20. Are we possibly focusing too much on the roles of the five ministry gifts in some of the current books and teachings on this subject?

Yes, I believe this is so. The roles weren't given by Jesus to provide positions for certain people in the church. This concept puts the emphasis upon the overseer instead of what needs to be overseen. That is clearly upside down. It also leads to possible aberrations of power-mongering and control, which have created a multitude of problems. Instead, we need to focus upon each of the flows these five roles are overseeing, upon the movement God wants each to have within the church.

21. What about elections of people into these roles? Can that work? Likewise, what does this mean for hiring?

First of all, we should know what mantle is required for each role when we are hiring or electing. Is it pastor, teacher, evangelist, apostle, or prophet that we are looking for? Secondly, we should be able to know who we're hiring or electing well enough to discern the anointing and calling that they have. Remember, the problems that can occur if we don't match up roles expected with the specific anointing and calling from God. We really need to be led by the Spirit in this.

22. What if a church doesn't have multiple staff and can't afford to hire so many people? How can this all work?

The two roles that are absolutely essential to the local church are pastor and teacher. Remember, although it's good to pay someone, it isn't necessary for every role. Many of those involved in the early church had jobs and served the church at the same time. Paul and his tent making is an example. Let me say, however, that the more people are fully supported, the more they can concentrate on their corresponding current. We have tended to give full-time pay only to pastors. No wonder the other currents aren't flowing so strongly.

Connections can be forged with strong teachers, evangelists, prophetic servants, and apostolic workers. It's ideal for a growing church to have a person who really loves evangelism and is comfortable with the wooing current. The prophetic voices may also be local, but there are also speakers who can be brought in who may be anointed for a stronger work. This is true of the apostolic emissaries. When these various folks visit, be sure to use them appropriately. They should be "training the people to do the work of the ministry" for their current.

There are people in every congregation with inclinations and a calling from God toward one or more of these currents. Note them and use them. Conscientiously allow each current to have some sort of oversight and spokesperson(s). Let them be at the table so their voices can be heard.

23. Historically, hasn't the emphasis on the pastoral role alone had an impact on the pastors?

I'm sad to say that it has. More than 1,700 pastors leave the ministry every month, and I believe that much of the burnout and stress caused by the pastorate is because the five currents are not flowing fully. We haven't recognized and nurtured all of the five ministry gifts. This has left pastors shouldering five times the responsibility and work that they should. Furthermore, this requires that they function in roles to which they haven't been called or received anointing and strength to fulfill. All the burdens of the church are upon one office rather than spread out upon a team of individuals representing different currents who can assist and encourage one another. This is totally exhausting for the pastor.

24. Should a church evaluate itself on these currents?

Yes, indeed, that's a great plan! These currents are the most important ones that God wants for a healthy church. If we desire revitalization and transformation, we must seek the Lord for His assessment of each current. We must pray, wait, and hear what He has to say. When He gives us eyes to discern spiritual effectiveness instead of numbers, programs, and activities, we're ready to ask Him the next question: What are we supposed to do about these currents that aren't flowing as fully as they should? We shouldn't be shocked if God asks us to put aside some current programming so we have the space to take on something new. And we shouldn't be surprised if He makes us wait in prayer for a while. He'll be at work; we needn't worry about that. He wants us to connect to Him first.

25. What happens when all five currents are flowing strongly?

Revival is what happens. Yes, whenever revivals have occurred historically, all five of these currents have been flowing. Their strength comes out of the revival. Furthermore, God raises up people to serve in all five roles As we come to know the details of the historical revivals, we can see the evangelist, the pastor, the teacher, the prophetic servant, and the apostolic emissary all working together. It's a joy to behold!

When God is free to move, as He is in revival, the Triune God brings a fresh flow of each and every current. The Trinity has been working in every one of them all along from the beginning, and the Three are all desirous of pouring out even more upon us. Will we receive it?

THINGS TO CONSIDER . . .

1. Are you one of the "some" whom God has called to be a particular gift to the church by overseeing a current? If so, which one? Have you shifted around in your roles?

2. If you aren't called to be an overseer, where do you think your calling might be in one of the currents to help support that current and contribute to its flow? Have you been trained to do your part?

3. Have you perhaps been called to work with a certain current but haven't realized it until reading this book? What are you going to do about that now?

4. What possible mix-ups do you see around you for people who are called by a certain gifting title but actually function best in a different one? What can be done about this?

5. How can we let all five of the gifts function on the leadership team or at least have input to the team?

6. How has the false, deceitful side of various gifting roles caused problems, and what can be done about it?

7. Do you think we're clearly focusing upon the five currents and not just upon those who are overseeing those currents?

8. What are some problems that occur when all five currents aren't functioning well? What might be lacking?

9. Do you believe revival is on the way?

ACKNOWLEDGEMENTS

Thanks to all those who reviewed the manuscript at an early stage and made such helpful comments and suggestions. These include Ken Draughon, Sherry Grams, Wendy Cunningham, Julie Temmel-Friesen, and Sarah Laulunen. Particular appreciation goes to Sheri Ray and Joe Girdler who provided thorough and unusually helpful feedback that helped in the forming of this book.

Love goes to my husband, Ray, who has always supported me in ministry, preaching, teaching, and writing, and whatever God calls me to do! Throughout the time I wrote this book I had three orthopedic surgeries in a row during which he fetched and aided beyond the call of duty. Without him this book would not have become a reality.

Special thanks go as well to my friends from Cohort 30 at the Assemblies of God Theological Seminary at Evangel University where I teach doctoral classes. They know better than anyone how they set about to make sure this book happened! I'm so glad you have a vision for this book, Ken Draughon, David Grant, and Joe Girdler along with so many others. I am also appreciative for my editor at My Healthy Church, Terri Gibbs, who sensed in the Spirit what needed to happen with this book.

ENDNOTES

Introduction

1. T. S. Elliot. "Little Gidding" in the *Four Quartets*, 1943. Columbia University website. http://www.columbia.edu/itc/history/winter/w3206/edit/tseliotlittlegidding.html (accessed 8/7/14).

Chapter 1 Living in a Coracle

2. Ian Bradley, *The Celtic Way* (London: Darton, Longman and Todd, 1993), 80.

3. Ibid., 77.

4. Ronald Ferguson, *George Macleod: Founder of the Iona Community* (London: HarperCollins, 1990), 123.

5. Brendan the Navigator. *Navigatio Sancti Brendani Abbatis*. MS Alençon. Trans. Carl Selmer. (Milwaukee: U of Notre Dame Press, 1959) ch. 5 accessed August 1, 2014 http://curragh.sakura.ne.jp/eng/navigatio-eng.html.

6. John O'Donohue. "Fluent" in *Conamara Blues* (HarperCollins e-books, 2009).

Chapter 3 The Powerful Wooing Current

7. My Church Growth. Accessed June 4, 2014 http://Mychurch growth.com/church%20growth/agr.php.

8. Steve McSwain. The Blog. October 14, 2013 "Why Nobody Wants to Go to Church Anymore." accessed June 6, 2014 http://www.huffingtonpost.com/steve-mcswain/why-nobody-wants-to-go-to_b_4086016.html

9. Pew Charitable Trust. Accessed June 5,2014 www.pewforum.org/2011/12/19/globalchristianity-exec/1.

10. American Sunday-School Union. (New York: Bible House, nd), 84 in *Missionary Anecdotes. Series First*, Making of America Digital Library, accessed September 19, 2014 http://quod.lib.umich.edu/m/moa/ajg7538.0001.001/96?page=root;sid=95e3f6e828e116b80d4cccd93c806bc1;size=100;view=image.

11. Billy Graham Evangelistic Association, "The Story of How God Called Billy Graham" accessed September 19, 2014 http://www.billygraham.org.uk/Groups/178966/Billy_Graham_Evangelistic/Who_We_Are/About_Us/Billy_Graham_History/Billy_Graham_History.aspx.

Chapter 4 The Evangelist

12. Leonard C. Albert, "Telling It Like It Is: Personal Evangelism and the Great Commission" in *The Great Commission Connection*, Raymond F. Culpepper, ed., (Cleveland, TN: Pathway Press, 2011), 521.

13. Ibid.

14. Chuck Miller, *The Spiritual Formation of Leaders: Integrating Spiritual Formation and Leadership Development*. (Maitland, FL: Xulon Press, 2007), Kindle e-book, location 3050.

Chapter 5 The Radical Forming Current

15. Dallas Willard, *The Great Omission: Reclaiming Jesus's Essential Teaching on Discipleship* (New York: HarperCollins e-books, 2014), 22.

16. Leonard Sweet, *I Am a Follower: The Way, Truth and Life of Following Jesus* (Nashville: Thomas Nelson, 2012), Kindle e-book, location 610.

Chapter 6 The Teacher

17. *The Great Omission*, 114.

18. *I Am a Follower*, Kindle e-book, location 510.

19. A. W. Tozer quotes, accessed July 24, 2014, http://www.quotes.net/quote/50829.

20. Smith Wigglesworth, *Smith Wigglesworth on Prayer*, ed. and comp. Larry Keefauver (Lake Mary, FL: Creation House, 1997), 36.

Chapter 7 The Synchronized Choreography Current

21. Alexandre Dumas, *The Three Musketeers* (New York: Modern Library Classics, Bantam Books, 2001).

22. Will Davis, Jr., *10 Things Jesus Never Said* (Ada, MI: Revell, 2011).

23. C. S. Lewis, *Perelandra* (New York: Scribner, 2003), 219.

24. Ibid., chapter 17.

25. Barna Group, (April 8, 2014) "The State of the Bible: 6 Trends for 2014" accessed June 25, 2014 https://www.barna.org/barna-update/culture/664-the-state-of-the-bible-6-trends-for-2014#.U9L_HYLL_Og.

26. John Ortberg, *Soul Keeping: Caring for the Most Important Part of You* (Grand Rapids: Zondervan, 2014) Kindle e-book, location 77.

27. Ray C. Steadman, *Body Life* (Glendale, CA: Regal, 1972), 26.

28. *The Spiritual Formation of Leaders*, Kindle e-book, location 3342.

29. Ibid., chapter 11.

30. http://www.brainyquote.com/quotes/quotes/d/dwight lmo386598.html

Chapter 8 The Pastor

31. *Smith Wigglesworth on Prayer*, 54.

32. St. Patrick, *Confession of St. Patrick*, Christian Classics Ethereal Library, accessed July 27, 2014 http://www.ccel.org/ccel/patrick/confession.html.

33. David Clark, "The Celtic Goose Is a Great Symbol of the Holy Spirit and for St. Luke's," May 31, 2009, St. Luke's Presbyterian Church, Aotearoa, NZ, accessed July 27, 2014 http://www.stlukes.org.nz/?sid=42258.

Chapter 9 The Directional Prophetic Current

34. J. R. R. Tolkien, *The Lord of the Rings, The Fellowship of the Rings* single vol. ed. Book One, Ch. II "The Shadow of the Past" (New York: Houghton Mifflin, 1993), 7.

Chapter 10 The Prophetic Servant

35. Adomnan, *Life of St. Columba, Founder of Hy*. Ed. William Reeve, Book I, "Of His Prophetic Revelations," Ch. XXXV (Edinburgh: Edmonston and Douglas, 1874). Fordham University website, Internet Medieval Sourcebook, accessed December 13, 2015 http://www.fordham.edu/halsall/basis/columba-e.asp.

Endnotes

Chapter 11 The Miraculous Sending Current

36. *Confession of St. Patrick.*

37. Unknown Author(s). *Annals of the Four Masters.* CELT (the Corpus of Electronic Texts), Ireland, accessed September 1, 2014 http://www.ucc.ie/celt/online/T100005A/.

38. Kardia Church Planting and Remissioning Blog. 3/17/2014 "St. Patrick and the Irish Way of Making Disciples," accessed September 1, 2014 http://www.kardiaanglican.com/kardia-blog/2014/5/15/saint-patrick-the-irish-way-of-making-disciples.

39. *Annals of the Four Masters.*

Chapter 12 The Apostolic Emissary

40. Tim Peters, "10 Real Reasons Pastors Quit Too Soon," *Church Leaders*, 2014, accessed September 1, 2014 http://www.churchleaders.com/pastors/pastor-articles/161343-tim_peters_10_common_reasons_pastors_quit_too_soon.html.

ABOUT THE AUTHOR

Carolyn Tennant, Ph.D., maintains an active speaking schedule around the United States and internationally. She ministers in district and national conferences, pastors' retreats, district councils and camps, women's events, and churches. Dr. Tennant served for nearly thirty years at North Central University in Minneapolis, Minnesota, where she was a professor and vice president. She is ordained in the Assemblies of God and presently is an adjunct professor teaching regularly in the doctor of ministry program at the Assemblies of God Theological Seminary of Evangel University in Springfield, Missouri.

FOR MORE INFORMATION

CATCH the WIND of the SPIRIT

How the 5 MINISTRY GIFTS *Can Transform Your Church*

Carolyn Tennant

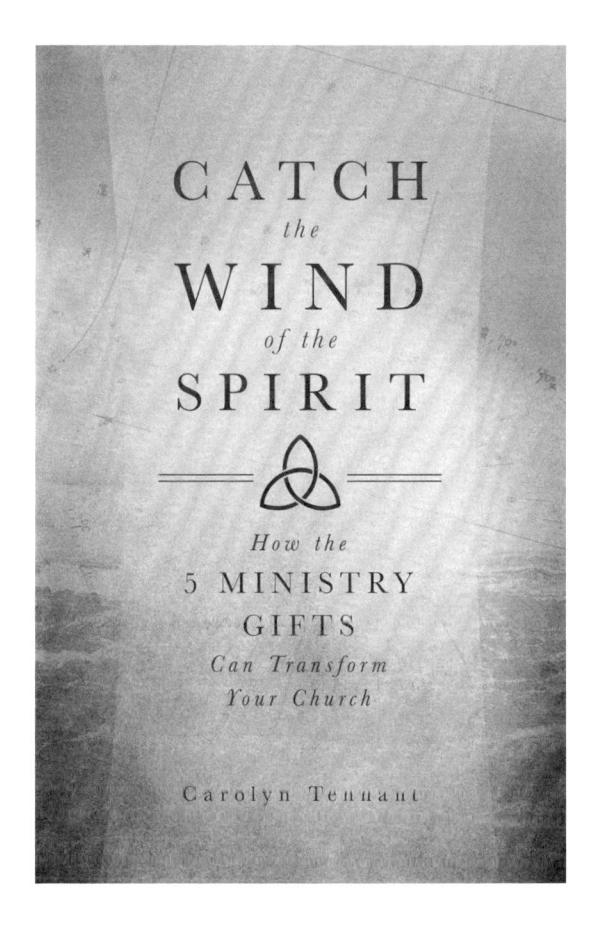

For more information on this and other valuable resources visit www.myhealthychurch.com.